With our compliments

The BEDFORD
CONSULTING
GROUP INC.

Keith

Keep this book in
mind for your
next role.

Russ.

THE PATH TO MASTERY

New Role, New Reality

How to deliver results when merger, acquisition, promotion, transfer, or a move to a new organization changes your world

John O. Burdett

New Role, New Reality
© Orxestra Inc., 2000

Published by:
Executive Forum, a division of Canada Forum Inc.
Toronto, Canada

Individual and bulk orders can be placed:
In Toronto (416) 925-0866
In North America 1-800-443-6452

Process orders on our website http://www.orxestra.com

ISBN# 0-9687233-0-6

Introduction

Introduction

Moving into a new role

R ecent research suggests that at least 40% of those moving in to a new role struggle. For CEO's the statistic is closer to 60%. At a time when it often takes up to a year to fill a key leadership role these are remarkable figures. Failure represents a major setback for the executives concerned and missed opportunity for the organization in question. In some instances failure can mean that the business itself is severely weakened.

There are a number of reasons why executives derail when they move into a new role. Inadequate definition of the role, poor recruitment practices and lack of openness during the hiring process all play their part. High on any list of why those moving into a new role stumble, however, is that they are given little or no support during the crucial integration period.

This omission is quite remarkable when you think about the overall cost of hiring, and/or the additional cost of having someone in a leadership role who is struggling to find his or her feet. The reality: the faster an executive integrates into the new role, the faster he or she can begin to produce value for the organization. The challenge: the time that an executive is given to prove him/herself is getting ever shorter. The rate of change, the speed at which the business world changes, leaves little room for someone sitting on the sidelines waiting to learn the plays.

Integration support also has a significant impact on leadership retention. Talented people stay with an organization for all sorts of reasons: the reputation of the organization, a sense of accomplishment, freedom to act, the feeling that he/she is making a difference. More important than anything else, however, is the quality of learning offered by the organization. It is a perception that is created, for better or for worse, as soon as a new executive joins the organization. For the established executive, that initial feeling is revisited every time he or she moves into a new role. Lack of support during those early and anxious days means not only a costly waiting period while the new executive gets up to speed, but it may well mean the loss of that executive the next time he or she is courted. At a time of dramatic shortfalls in leadership talent, these are business issues that cannot be ignored.

In talking about executive integration we are not limited to those who move between organizations – although this is an important issue. Merger and acquisition means that many of the key roles change, and change dramatically. An organization going through what is often referred to as "culture change" of necessity redefines the role of every leader in the organization. A move to another country even where, at first glance, the work seems to be the same, invariably means that the role has changed. Promotion, internal transfer and new leadership challenge mean that the leader in question has to think anew his or her role.

Need executive integration be problematical? Need there be a 40% failure rate? The answer is a resounding NO! Having said that, without a new approach, little will change. A better way is possible only if the organization introduces the tools that allow the new executive to take responsibility for his or her own integration. Equally important, a better way is possible only where the new executive is given a clear path to follow.

This book was written to meet that need. My material comes directly from working with executives moving into new roles. The content draws on direct personal experience either as a consultant or as a management development professional. It is an experience base that encompasses work on five continents and at all levels of organizational life.

Those who successfully move into a new role quickly realize that flexibility, openness and a willingness to learn are the name of the game. The book encourages the reader to step back and become the observer of his/her own behavior, to ask new questions and to draw new insights from the experience. A summary, key questions to support reflection, and an action plan are outlined at the end of each chapter to enrich the overall learning that can be taken from the book.

What are the recommendations about using this book? From those who have worked with the material, three suggestions emerge. One group found value in reading the book before moving into the new role. When they actually moved into the new role the material took on the nature of a field-book that could be accessed when and as they came up against a problem.   The contents page is written in a way that supports this approach. A second group used the material as a workbook. Their feedback was that they got the greatest value by (1) establishing an integration time-line and (2) working their way through the book systematically. A third group described the book as "very rich" but drew on only those chapters that addressed issues where they felt they needed to do more work.

In large measure, how the book is used is a matter of learning style and experience. It is worth noting that a number of those who have been through the material said that they wished they had had the book before **accepting** the new role. Here the suggestion was that if they had read the book they would have been better equipped to make a decision on whether the new role was a good fit.

The word "executive" is peppered throughout this book. Not so long ago this would have applied only to a relatively small group of "top" people. Today, with the flattening of organizational structures, the pushing of decision-making closer to the customer, the term "executive" should rightfully be applied to anyone who has the opportunity to shape the nature and breadth of their contribution.   For those who would be more comfortable doing so, the word *leader* can be substituted for the term *executive* wherever and whenever it appears in the text.

Executives, in the modern organization, thus do not necessarily carry glamorous titles or operate out of a prestigious office along mahogany row.   An executive is simply someone who, through initiative, creativity and a willingness to act, makes a significant difference to the way the company creates value for its customers.   Using this definition means that executives can be found at every level and in all parts of the organization.

The term "hiring executive" is used throughout the text. This definition is used to describe the "manager" one level up. In some situations he or she may not actually be the person who made the hire decision e.g. he or she was hired at the same time as you. "Team leader" was an alternative choice but is potentially confusing in that today's executive is on a number of different teams. "Boss" was rejected because it carries with it thoughts of hierarchy and "bosship."

How long should the integration take? This is a difficult question because, in the classic words of a successful consultant, "It all depends." As a rough guide – and assuming that the reader has been through the entire text - someone moving into a new role should **work on** the issues contained on a schedule that would cover at least one chapter a week. Having said that, in many businesses a month is an awful long time.

Executive integration is an important issue. It is also a practical issue. If you have just moved into a new role you cannot afford to fail. If you are the hiring executive you cannot afford anything less than total success.

The Model

The Model

In most books the underlying architecture is like the steelwork that supports a building – although essential it remains unseen.

In New Role, New Reality the explicit model that shapes the content is revisited at the beginning of each chapter. There are several reasons for this. The first is that a conceptual map of the reader's journey can add significantly to the underlying learning. For some, there is lasting value in being able to see, from the outset, how all of the pieces fit together.

A second reason is that the underlying structure reveals the thinking that lies behind the material. Integration is played out through an ongoing tension between expectations and fit. Fit describes the need to build meaningful relationships with three important constituencies: the hiring executive, the team and the wider organization. The wider organization in this context includes the customer. Managing expectations goes through three distinct stages: testing reality (is this where I really want to be), setting the stage (agreeing on what has to be accomplished), and starting to deliver. Delivering fit and managing expectations are the music and the steps of the integration process. A focus on one to the exclusion of the other leads to critical issues during the integration process being missed. Each chapter in the book describes a critical phase of this ongoing dance.

A third reason for presenting the integration model is that, in addition to those faced with a new role, the target audience for this book includes the hiring executive, human resource professionals, outplacement consultants, and executive search practitioners. Their respective roles will be to support someone moving into a new role. For them, the book becomes a means to build common language with the individual they are working with, and the integration model a container that frames and supports the ongoing dialogue.

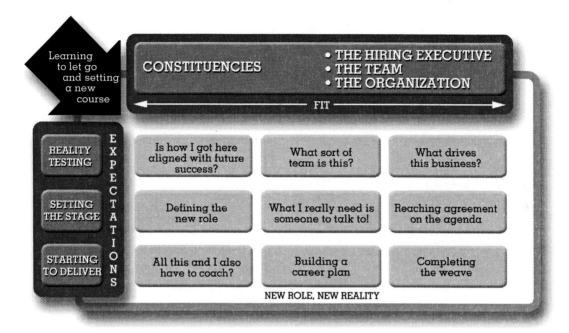

A final reason for the model is that material has significance beyond that defined by the title. Leadership programs, teambuilding initiatives, discussions on strategy, coaching, issues of culture, for example, can all be enriched if those involved read through the appropriate chapter. In unbundling the material contained, however, something of the overall gestalt is lost. This deficit is significantly reduced if the reader takes two or three minutes to reflect on the broader context from which the material is drawn.

Contents

Contents

Contents

Learning to let go and setting a new course

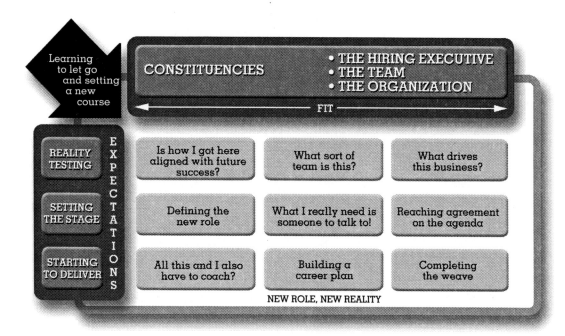

Learning to let go and setting a new course

CONSTITUENCIES
- THE HIRING EXECUTIVE
- THE TEAM
- THE ORGANIZATION

FIT

EXPECTATIONS

REALITY TESTING	Is how I got here aligned with future success?	What sort of team is this?	What drives this business?
SETTING THE STAGE	Defining the new role	What I really need is someone to talk to!	Reaching agreement on the agenda
STARTING TO DELIVER	All this and I also have to coach?	Building a career plan	Completing the weave

NEW ROLE, NEW REALITY

Learning to let go and setting a new course

"It's an honor just to be nominated." Being wooed by a prestigious executive search company can give anyone a warm feeling. Even those who are happy in their present organization find that being courted can do wonders for the ego. Promotion within your present organization is equally gratifying – there's pride in being recognized and the confidence of others can go a long way toward enhancing your own self-confidence. And there is value in the interview process itself: it forces one to take the time to be introspective about career progress, marketability and personal needs, and provides you with a discerning and informed listener.

The down side is the inconvenience. It takes time out of a busy schedule. It may involve flying to a different city or, these days, country. It means doing research. It usually means several interviews. And then there are the inevitable questions: where is my new tie? Do these earrings go?

An internal change of role is no less time consuming. Moving internally is also typically done in the absence of the professional middleman, so support is less explicit. The results for the shifted executive can be confusion, stress, a feeling of isolation, and inefficiency.

Then comes decision day, probably better named doubt day. Is this a good move? Will I be happy? Perhaps more important: is this a role I can succeed in? Some make the decision purely on gut: does it feel right? Others enter into a frenzy of phone calls, research, and navel gazing. Both approaches are probably worthwhile. Both can reduce the risk of failure. But neither really equip the candidate for the new role. Moving into a new position is something like skydiving; planning and preparing are essential, but, no matter how thorough, they still don't prepare you for what it feels like to actually jump.

On the way down from the plane, the excitement of the jump is inevitably overtaken by a realization that the landing zone looks strange and uneven. All of a sudden you realize that

Chapter 1

*Learning to let
go and setting
a new course*

over to the left is a large hole filled with muddy water — and you in your new shoes! Where'd this wind come from? No one mentioned these frequent gusts. And everywhere else, silence! Where's that guy that coached you out the door?

Then there is the landing. Even those who have made many jumps can crash on landing. Executives faced with a new role will, if forced to be candid, confess to experiencing a range of emotions, most of them negative. Words like "confusing," "chaotic," "frustrating," and "overwhelming" come mixed with phrases like "there is no one to talk to," "you wouldn't believe how they...."

Put simply, moving into or assuming a new role is a difficult period in any executive's working life, and he or she enters into the new situation feeling profoundly at risk. Get it right, successfully scramble through the early days, and the feelings of inadequacy quickly fade. Get it wrong and those early negative impressions concerning the organization and his or her place within it, will be very difficult to overcome. A few wrong turns during the integration period can take an executive off the corporate map and into hostile territory.

Getting the best out of the integration opportunity is really about **attitude**. It is about emotional commitment and being willing to see what others describe as a burden, as a rich learning experience. The real spirit, and thus mastery, of executive integration lies in the belief that confusion, frustration and occasional bouts of depression are merely the price to pay for **a unique opportunity to better know one's self**.

The good news is executive integration doesn't have to be a debilitating experience. It need not be a combination of scavenger hunt and obstacle course. Those who have framed each integration experience as a self-development opportunity, those who have found the techniques for coping and the strategies for achieving, have discovered that success in a new role is ultimately a process that, like any other, can be learned.

Without getting too poetic, a worthwhile integration process unfolds much like a flower when it receives sunlight. The flower cannot move into full bloom, however, unless the soil is rich enough to sustain its growth. The nurturing mix that sustains the integration process is emotional discipline and positive self-analysis — characteristics that are critical to the first stage of integration: Letting Go and Setting a New Course.

This first stage of moving into a new role is not an element of the process that once completed can be set aside. Those going through the integration process inevitably find themselves falling back into old ways of thinking and behaving. The executive will be tempted, simply because of his or her new workload, to put integration as a specific activity on the back burner. Doing so allows those old patterns to re-emerge. The reality: energizing the integration process is an ever-present challenge.

To enable him or herself to let go and get going, there are several key elements the executive must address very early on in his or her new role. **See Figure 1**.

Lack of integration support

One might look to a number of people and places for support during a change in role. Clearly the search consultant - assuming there is one – should play a role, as should the Human Resource executive involved. The hiring executive has a strong vested interest. Colleagues, subordinates and customers also have a stake in the new executive's success. Yet, there is really only one place where responsibility rests, only one person to whom failure can be a lasting setback, and only one person who can truly make it happen: the executive who as a result of transfer, promotion, acquisition, merger, selection, or simply as a consequence of ongoing change, finds that he/she is faced with the reality of success in a new role. Others *can and should* provide support. A mentor can be the source of new questions and insights. The hiring executive can help identify potholes in the road ahead. But only the new executive is in the position to put it all together.

To make the integration period a productive and lasting learning experience it is a good idea for the new executive to keep a diary or journal. By jotting down feelings, thoughts and questions he/she is doing much to set in place the

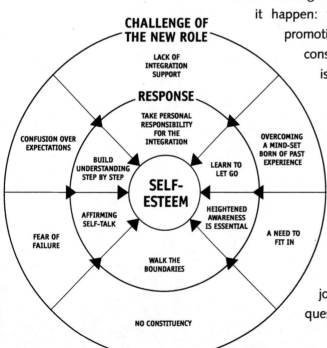

Figure 1

Chapter 1

*Learning to let
go and setting
a new course*

underlying architecture needed for meaningful, ongoing reflection. Reflection is an essential part of any learning experience and something that few in business practise. Without reflection, important insights are overlooked, feelings get lost and the quality of any periodic assessment of progress is significantly diminished.

But let's also not undervalue the emotional practicality of the diary – it's a great way to blow off steam. The act of writing down and capturing emotions, negative thoughts, and frustration goes a long way toward purging them. And, once written down, those same thoughts can be reviewed, away from the heat of the battle, with a more balanced frame of mind.

Overcoming a mind-set based on past experience

When the law of the jungle governed life, primitive man survived by developing the ability to switch part of his awareness to "auto-pilot". The modern version of this is driving to work and being totally unaware, at a conscious level at least, of the journey itself. Our ancestors developed this capacity in order that part of their attentive powers could be held in readiness should they find that they had an unexpected appointment with a certain Mr. Saber Tooth. To run on auto-pilot, however, meant that man and his evolutionary mate evolved a somewhat restricted repertoire of behaviors when dealing with that which was new. The inherited result is that man has not evolved in a way that allows him or her to deal easily with change at the speed witnessed by those operating in today's jungle. As for the tigers, well, they're still around.

In *The Forest People* (1962), Colin Turnbull writes of the Pygmy people living in the Ituri Forest in the Congo. He tells a wonderful story of a young man named Kenge, who took his first trip out of the forest in the company of Turner. On seeing buffalo grazing several miles away, the young pygmy asked Turner: "What are those insects?" Kenge had never seen things from the viewpoint of the unending grassland. Thousands of generations of forest life, where the furthest thing he or his ancestors looked upon was literally only a few feet away, had resulted in his sense of the world being devoid of any notion of perspective.

Our orientation, our current ways of behaving, our mind-sets (mental models) regarding a new role, are the outcome of a series of competing emotional forces:

- What worked in the past.
- The executive's view of an ideal future.
- Early signals about what success looks like.
- The executive's values and beliefs.
- Role models from previous business experience.

During the integration process the new executive is operating at a heightened level of awareness. This intense sense of the new reality is both necessary and, paradoxically, potentially damaging. Necessary because the new executive is after all crossing new terrain. Potentially damaging because as a direct result of this heightened sense, insecurity starts to creep in and with it the propensity to default in favor of past behavior. What is often misunderstood is the extent to which what worked in the past can be, and often is, a barrier to developing new ways to act and think.

The implications for those moving into a new role are profound. Previous experience and past assumption of success become the filters through which new opportunities are judged. Established ways to be and past solutions become the "established tools of the trade" and are presumed to have primacy regardless of the situation.

By way of example it is not at all unusual for executives even a year or more into a new role to continue to refer to past experience as the basis for proposed change in the new organization: "Let me tell you how we did this in my past organization." In doing so, the individual concerned is not only unknowingly alienating their new colleagues, but through their frames of reference telling others, "I'm not sure if I want to be part of this team." The message they give out is that their head and their hand may be committed to the new role but their heart and spirit lies elsewhere.

The challenge: moving forward (getting going) is only possible if **preceded by** the act of letting go: letting go of past failures that inhibit future risk, letting go of past practices, letting go of established solutions, and letting go of prejudicial assumptions (e.g. "engineers are...," "the union always..."). Assumptions about how speed and integrity are defined, about the role of the corporate office, and about the meaning of management

Chapter 1

*Learning to let
go and setting
a new course*

tools such as TQM, process reengineering, strategic planning, and empowerment, equally, all need to be thought through anew.

The new executive must also be willing to let go of language, especially metaphors that present imagery that is misaligned with the new culture. Metaphors that strike male images ("we have to put the puck in the net this time") in an environment where a high percentage of the team are women; win-lose language ("kill the competition") where the business environment is one highly dependent upon alliances; and language that frames performance as being the prerogative of individual success but where the climate is one highly dependent upon the team ("when the ice is thin success goes to the fastest skater") all serve to set the new executive apart, all significantly limit what is possible. For a leader language isn't merely important - language is everything! Language gives potency to an idea, language energizes, language engages, language provides meaning, and language translates concepts into action. But only if it is the *right language!* We will revisit language in Chapter two.

A need to fit in

Deep in man's nature is a need to belong. The family, the tribe, the village, the community have always figured significantly in our history. Little that is in our nature fits with the notion of man as the lone hunter riding off alone, save for his trusty steed, into the setting sun.

Examples of man as a communal animal abound. The worst censure that unionized workers can impose on one of their colleagues is to ostracize him or her. Many managers and others following redundancy "strike out on their own." Some succeed. But most languish in a world of uncertainty desperately seeking a team to belong to. When faced with a challenge that takes us to the very edge of our comfort zone most of us ask the same question: "Where's Tonto?" It's not a lot of fun being the **Lone** Ranger.

Integration, when everything else is stripped away, is about two things: the ability to fit in and the ability to manage expectations. Inappropriate behavior with regard to either can lead to difficulties. Managing expectations ultimately comes down to the nature, quality and timing of delivery. Fit is another matter altogether.

Fit is largely to do with overall presentation, personal style, orientation, language and pace. The higher the quality of the gem, the more time and effort needs to be spent on crafting the setting. Fit begins as an issue before the start date for the new role. Fit is a feature of the integration equation from the very first time there is contact. It is a product of trust, sensitivity and, above all else, awareness. From the very first interaction the new executive needs to have his/her antennae fully extended. An outstanding salesman or saleswoman does this naturally. Indeed, top sales people are the grand masters of political astuteness. Similarly, the new executive needs to become quickly attuned to his or her new political and social environment.

Past experience can be both a source of strength, and the source of what often amounts to a skewed view of the new reality. Some specialists, for example, are invariably skilled at identifying the fiscal or technical issues but lack judgment when it comes to people. And make no mistake, fit is a "people issue".

There are many things that the new executive should be assessing. The following questions, however, loom high in any assessment of fit: how does this organization create value for its customers? Does moving into the new role entail, for me, new ways to think? To act? To feel? How is the company organized? Is there a well-defined strategy? What is it? What stories are being told? What systems dominate? What values are implied by the behavior I come across? What gets measured? How do teams act? What is the commitment to teamwork? How do teams communicate with other teams? How do key individuals behave? What seems to drive them? What do they talk about? Where, and on what, is there a real focus (discipline)?

Fit is a two-way process. Starting to understand what drives the organization and how people behave is not the same as fit. The new executive needs to not only be conscious of how others behave but be acutely aware of his or her own actions. He or she needs to put him or herself into the shoes of those he or she meets and ask how does this person perceive me? What sort of individual does he or she think I am?

The ability to see the world as someone else does is referred to, in NeuroLinguistic programming, as being able to move from first to second position. First position is seeing the world through "my" eyes - something men are particularly prone to do. Second position is

Chapter 1

*Learning to let
go and setting
a new course*

the ability to move into someone else's body and see the world from their point of view. There is a third position: the ability to step back from the ongoing communication and become both participant and observer. In third position, the individual displays an ability to interpret the ongoing interpersonal dance, and anticipate moves in order to lead or follow as desired.

Fit is the positive outcome of heightened awareness. Fit is about listening. It is, ultimately, about making personal adjustment - something that is highly unlikely if the new executive is stuck in first position. Gathering information is a first position attribute. Awareness, knowing **and** acting with purpose, are possible only if the new executive moves comfortably and elegantly, as needed, through all three positions.

No constituency

A move into a new role is a little like traveling to a new country. At the point of departure everything is compatible. The language is easy to understand and if something goes wrong knowing how to get it fixed is relatively straightforward. Upon arrival, everything changes. There is a new language to contend with. There are new customs and new ways to get things done. Even the police can't be assumed to have the same priorities. The likelihood is that even the climate will be different. And if the plane is delayed and plans have been disrupted, panic is a not uncommon response.

Arrival is a far less stressful experience if a friend or colleague who knows the environment is waiting on the tarmac. With an intra-company move that is indeed a possibility. For an executive moving into a new organization it is far less likely.

For a politician to get elected and hold power, he or she must have a constituency of support. For executives to even start to compete at the highest level they too must be given support. Without a network even the brightest and best executives are destined to get lost. Without a constituency the new executive will feel as if they've wandered into a constantly reconfiguring maze.

A constituency, of course, is exactly what the new executive **doesn't** have. He or she, therefore, needs to build one - an untenable goal if the new executive sits in his or her office waiting for the world to knock on the door.

As early as possible in the role, then, the new executive needs to walk the boundaries of the new frontier. Peers and those in similar roles elsewhere in the organization should be high on the get-to-know list, but, equally, customers and suppliers need to become familiar to the executive in a new role. Outlying manufacturing operations or branch offices are likewise an invaluable source of information.

Your constituency supports you, but in order for them to remain your constituency, they must believe that you support them in return. To this end, here are a few points of constituency-building advice for the new executive visiting other parts of the operation:

- Find the time.
- On domestic flights, don't travel first or business class if other members of your team travel coach.
- No surprise first visits. The first visit to any part of the organization should be arranged ahead of time.
- Be punctual!
- Stick to soft drinks at lunch unless you happen to be meeting with a sales representative from Seagrams.
- Remember, those who control the access to power are often more important than those who wield it.
- If the visit was scheduled for two hours, stay two hours. Executives live in a goldfish bowl: cutting short a visit will leave people with the impression that you think they don't warrant your time; they will be disappointed, possibly resentful, and certainly nervous.
- People are as interested in the new executive as he or she is in them. Don't dominate, but share. Talk about your family. Be human. Under no circumstances, however, compare previous operations or experience with what it is you have found. This can cause resentment that may be very difficult to fix.
- The ultimate secret to constituency building is to be interested, not interesting. Look interested, act interested, be interested. Ask questions. Be curious. Be modest.
- Treat the visit and those you meet as if the reverse was actually taking place and it was your first visit to the hiring executive's home.

- Don't be critical no matter how tempted. On the other hand, don't be supportive of something you disagree with.

- Even if true, avoid words that suggest the visit is not your highest priority, as in "I *only* have a few minutes." Language that suggests distracted or short attention devalues the worth of the person being visited.

- Listen, listen, listen.

Fear of failure

It has been said that the first casualty of war is truth. For those wrestling with the complexities of a new role, the primary casualty is more likely self-esteem.

After being on top of his or her game in one organization or in a key position within the same organization, the executive in a new role is not only faced with the challenge of starting again as a beginner, but, worse yet, he or she is likely to discover that the other players are playing by the rules of a different game.

As self-esteem erodes so does the confidence to act. Nathaniel Branden, someone who has been studying and writing about self-esteem for twenty-five years, says: "When self-esteem is low, we are often manipulated by fear. Fear of reality, to which we feel inadequate. Fear of the facts about ourselves - or others - that we have denied, disowned, or repressed. Fear of exposure. Fear of the humiliation of failure and, sometimes, the responsibility of success. We live more to avoid pain than to experience joy." (*Six Pillars of Self-Esteem*, pg. 49).

As an example, **Figure 2** outlines different paths taken by those going through executive out-placement. Not only do those with high self-esteem

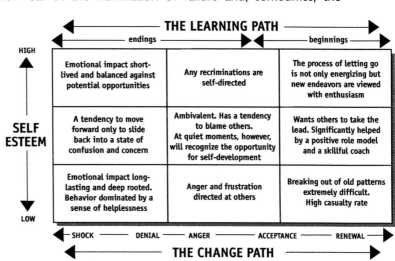

	THE LEARNING PATH	
endings		*beginnings*
Emotional impact short-lived and balanced against potential opportunities	Any recriminations are self-directed	The process of letting go is not only energizing but new endeavors are viewed with enthusiasm
A tendency to move forward only to slide back into a state of confusion and concern	Ambivalent. Has a tendency to blame others. At quiet moments, however, will recognize the opportunity for self-development	Wants others to take the lead. Significantly helped by a positive role model and a skillful coach
Emotional impact long-lasting and deep rooted. Behavior dominated by a sense of helplessness	Anger and frustration directed at others	Breaking out of old patterns extremely difficult. High casualty rate

SELF ESTEEM — HIGH / LOW

SHOCK ——— DENIAL ——— ANGER ——— ACCEPTANCE ——— RENEWAL

THE CHANGE PATH

Figure 2

cast off negative thinking quickly but, in sharp contrast to those approaching the task with low self-esteem, they find the process of letting go and moving ahead energizing. For those with a less positive self-image, anger and a need to recreate their past life are an ever present barrier that only skillful counseling can address.

———————— SELF-ESTEEM ————————

safety of the familiar (limited choices)	1. 2. 3. 4. 5. 6. 7. 8. 9. 10.	drawn to stretch goals – self-reliance
wounded by failure, or fear of failure	1. 2. 3. 4. 5. 6. 7. 8. 9. 10.	willing to admit mistakes – energized by failure
defend the comfort zone – control	1. 2. 3. 4. 5. 6. 7. 8. 9. 10.	drive to experience life
accepting of abuse and exploitation	1. 2. 3. 4. 5. 6. 7. 8. 9. 10.	high respect of self, high respect for others
looking for approval	1. 2. 3. 4. 5. 6. 7. 8. 9. 10.	affirming of others
a need to be better than someone else	1. 2. 3. 4. 5. 6. 7. 8. 9. 10.	the joy of being who you are
a need to be right – self-justification	1. 2. 3. 4. 5. 6. 7. 8. 9. 10.	a drive to explore the possibilities, self-expression, creativity
learning as a means to avoid failure	1. 2. 3. 4. 5. 6. 7. 8. 9. 10.	learning as a natural way of life

BASED ON ORIGINAL RESEARCH BY NATHANIEL BRANDEN

Figure 3

Figure 3 outlines the emotional choices faced by an executive in a new role. Those with low self-esteem, those who lack self-confidence, those who have little to draw on from their bank account of self-conviction, are inextricably drawn to the negative side of the model. Self-talk, the conversations we have with ourselves, can either affirm or limit our opportunity to act differently.

Pessimism is self-fulfilling. How we think is how we will feel. Fortunately we can learn how to argue with ourselves.

In *Learned Optimism*, Martin Seligman suggests there are a number of ways that people can deal with their pessimistic beliefs. Drawn out of extensive research, tactics that Seligman suggests are:

- Be aware of self-talk and write down negative thoughts. Revisit the comments at a set time later in the day.

Chapter 1

*Learning to let
go and setting
a new course*

- Challenge negative beliefs by looking for evidence. We say to ourselves "I can't learn French" and, if we say it often enough, it becomes a self-fulfilling prophecy. To avoid this we need to dispute such negative self-talk and ask of ourselves: "Where is the evidence for that?"

- *Decatastrophizing* the assertion. Even if the belief is true, it is important to ask: "What's the worst that can happen?"

Self-esteem is a major factor in each dimension of the integration model. No one is without self-doubt. None of us are complete. We are, at best, in the process of being. Life is a learning journey for both Lord Mayor and those who clean up after the show. Those moving into a new role need to understand that occasional moments of inner turmoil are perfectly normal (and can in fact be productive). The challenge is to not dwell on negative feelings to the point where they become self-fulfilling.

Confusion over expectations

It is impossible not to be awe-struck by the sheer size of the Great Wall of China. It is the only man-made structure easily visible from space. Most remarkable about the Wall is that it was built piecemeal. The skilled mason assigned to supervise the construction of several hundred yards of wall would, when his section was completed, return home to spend time with his family. After this "down time," the mason began a new construction at an entirely different location. Only later were the gaps in the wall filled in. It was built this way because the scarcest of the resources necessary for the construction of the wall were the skilled masons. Spending a lifetime in a remote part of China away from their families and on a task that they couldn't hope to see completed was found to be so demoralizing that a different strategy evolved. The joy and adulation his family and village showered on him at his return, coupled with the variety of work locations, invigorated and reestablished the mason's enthusiasm (*The Basic Kafka*, pg. 66-80).

This is not to suggest that integration as a process is a task of such colossal proportions that the new executive won't see it through in his or her lifetime (although at times it may feel that way). The story of the Wall illustrates that complex tasks are best tackled by breaking them down into smaller constituent parts. The integration process is no different.

Fit describes an appropriate style, a comfortable way to interact, building a network, and establishing trust as critical elements in establishing a constituency.

The ability to manage expectations is ultimately about performance, about doing what has been agreed upon. Managing expectations, however, is about more than just "winning." It is equally about the quality of performance, about **how** the new executive delivers the results.

Cultural fit, leadership, role definition, competency and values are all part of this, but we'll get to those in later chapters. The qualitative aspect of managing expectations, however, is important as soon as the new executive takes the stage in the new role. He or she must be aware of the "how" factor from day one. A good place to start: the organization's decision to hire.

Posing the question as to why the new executive was hired seems, at first blush, redundant. After all, he or she was hired because a job needed to be done. An opportunity existed and the best candidate was selected.

Life, of course, is never that simple, and uncovering the **thinking behind** the hire decision is an important first step in the new executive's insight into expectations.

The reason for the hire or promotion decision may have its genesis in any number of scenarios: is this a new position? If not, what happened to the previous player? Was he or she successful? If so, what qualities did he or she display that created that impression? Did the incumbent leave under a cloud? If so, what was the problem or issue? Is the job what Peter Drucker calls a "widow maker"? In other words, have several people failed in this role? Was the role redefined prior to the new executive being selected? What has changed, been added and/or taken away, in the process of the redefinition?

The answers to these questions can provide insights into the thinking that went into creating the job opening. The details gathered in answering these questions will help the executive determine the underlying criteria of success for the new role.

If a search firm was involved in the hire decision, the new executive has a valuable resource. Less seasoned search firms will be cautious about sharing information. Images

Chapter 1

*Learning to let
go and setting
a new course*

of libel suits or a need to legally validate their professional opinion will swirl into their mind. The real professionals, on the other hand, will be only too pleased to share their insights. After all, the more successful their selected candidate is in the new role, the better the search firm's relationship with client.

The new executive might look for information about what it was that suggested that he or she met the client's expectations. Where did the search consultant think his or her background or overall qualities were soft?

Discussion with the search professional should remain at the level of friendly dialogue. Requests for copies of interviews and/or other support materials encroach on the relationship the search company has with their client. Sunshine laws in some US states notwithstanding, asking for documentation that the search group considers confidential is not only going to make the search professional uncomfortable, but it is likely to alienate a valuable ally in the integration process.

Talking to the human-resource practitioner involved in the hire decision can be equally fruitful. Their vantage from within can provide much information about process and history that can give the executive in a new role a clearer picture of desires and expectations. Such a conversation can also be a real opportunity for the new executive to build a relationship with someone in a linchpin role.

Another strategy is a meeting with the outgoing executive. This is likely to be especially useful if the outgoing executive has joined another organization. But there is need for caution here. The new executive must carefully weigh the words of an outgoing executive.

And of course there is the hiring executive. Any steps taken by the executive in a new role should keep him or her involved and, above all else, informed.

After dwelling positively on the need to let go and the issues important to setting a new course, the new executive has to move quickly into considerations of culture, the topic of the next chapter.

Chapter One

Critical Learning

- The executive must take charge of his or her own integration into the new role.
- Past experience becomes the filter through which the new context is judged.
- Fit is largely to do with presentation, personal style, orientation, language and pace.
- Fear of failure impacts self-esteem. Self-esteem, in turn, impacts the confidence to act.
- Complex tasks are best approached by breaking them down into small constituent parts.
- The executive moving into a new role needs to understand the thinking behind the hire decision.

Consequences

Moving into a new role demands that the executive in question sees the world anew. Past practices, assumptions and a mind-set drawn out of previous experience have to be set aside. Unless the new executive is acutely aware of this, unless he or she is conscious of his or her behavior and how it impacts others, much of the early goodwill, and with it the opportunity to build a constituency, is lost.

Chapter 1

*Learning to let
go and setting
a new course*

Step back and reflect on the ideas that surfaced and the learning you take from this chapter. Consider the path you are on, the need to build relationships (fit), and your understanding of success in the new role (expectations). Think about what you need to stop doing, start doing, and that which you need to do differently.

_____

_____

_____

_____

_____

_____

_____

_____

_____

_____

_____

Is how I got here aligned with future success?

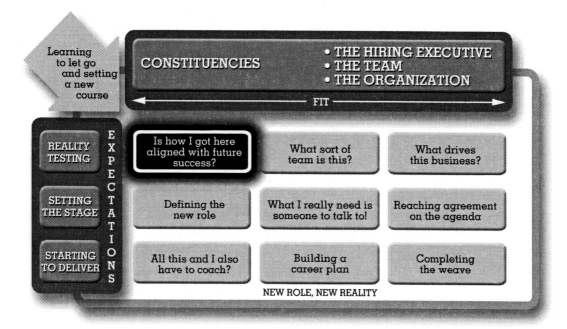

Learning to let go and setting a new course

CONSTITUENCIES
- **THE HIRING EXECUTIVE**
- **THE TEAM**
- **THE ORGANIZATION**

FIT

EXPECTATIONS			
REALITY TESTING	Is how I got here aligned with future success?	What sort of team is this?	What drives this business?
SETTING THE STAGE	Defining the new role	What I really need is someone to talk to!	Reaching agreement on the agenda
STARTING TO DELIVER	All this and I also have to coach?	Building a career plan	Completing the weave

NEW ROLE, NEW REALITY

Is how I got here aligned with future success?

Promotion within an organization, recruitment from outside, or being asked to move into an expanded role all serve to reinforce the past achievements of the new executive. Take time to absorb and enjoy that compliment. Okay, time's up. Now, you have to start to think hard about the new world you are entering, even if all that has changed is a single word on your business card. Whether you are remaining within your previous organization or moving into another, entering a new role means beginning anew – approach the new role by determining the nature of the culture that supports it. You've succeeded in the past, or else you wouldn't be here, but the strategies that got you here might not ensure your future success.

An executive moving into a new role needs to possess the kinds of skills typically found in a Scotland Yard detective. Finding your way in the new organization will require a careful reading of the "clues." Many of the clues are, of course, in plain view: the history of profitability, working capital, return on earnings, what the compensation system rewards, the identity of the key suspects…sorry, customers. But other information necessary to solving this case lies hidden; that is, unless the executive in question has the eye, ear, and intuitive sense to critically appraise what others simply see as the familiar. The quest: to determine how things *really* happen here. Who seems to succeed? Where are, and who holds, the levers of power?

Maybe the detective analogy is too loaded; it suggests you're looking for a crime and someone to expose as guilty, and that's the wrong way to go in. Perhaps a cultural anthropologist, or, in this case, an organizational anthropologist, might be a more accurate model for the new executive's behavior.

Look carefully at your work environment and analyze what its "culture" suggests about the people who made it that way (even if you are one of the people who made it that way). The simple act of coming into the building can supply a wealth of information about a company.

Who parks where? Do executives or customers have the prime parking spaces? Did your parking spot change when you were promoted? How are people dressed? Is this place informal or do suits dominate? What is the racial and ethnic mix? What seems to be the average age? What is the energy level of those in key roles? Are people smiling and upbeat or downcast?

Leaders concerned about morale can find out a great deal more than is ever revealed in an expensive climate survey by simply watching employees arrive at work. Executives joining a new organization need to be particularly attuned to this. It can be a pretty depressing experience to realize that those same down in the mouth, lackluster, "I wish I was someplace else," employees are about to be released on the customer. It is even more depressing to find that those who work for the competition deliver themselves to their own workplace with a sense of playful exuberance.

The building your organization occupies can also be revealing. Whether this is your first day, or if you've been coming here for years, step back and read the details for what they say about your organization and those working there. Is the building bright, uplifting and energetic? Does it feel like a hospital (but it's not a hospital)? What's the dominant color? What is on the notice boards? Do the notice boards describe business performance in a clear and lucid fashion? Is the share price and history of stock movement featured? Do managers and executives have separate offices, or does the environment reflect a high regard for teamwork? How is the workspace organized? What artifacts do people have in their personal spaces?

Those who value organization learning as a competitive imperative suggest that there is a collective consciousness within an organization that transcends the mere mortals who work there; something that is apparent even when the workplace is devoid of people. The use of space, color, symbolism, artifacts, and the posted notices combine (for better or worse) to provide the context and energy for the ongoing learning experience. On a slightly different note, the Chinese go further, believing that the design of the building, its shape, and its relationship to the space around it (Feng Shui) have a profound influence on the fortunes of those who work there.

For the executive turned cultural anthropologist, the opportunity to learn grows even richer as he or she meets those he or she will work with. Language is as valuable to the new executive as fingerprints to a forensics expert. The executive in a new role, whether in a new organization or within a familiar one, will do well to stop and listen to the way people talk about what they do – the language we choose reveals a great deal about the way we see ourselves. Is the language that of the warrior? "We have to make a beach head." "Take no prisoners." Conversely, organizations where the levers of power lie with those who see the business as a series of numbers frame the world as a series of quantitative problems: "If we address the margins we can solve this problem." "We have to get better metrics on this issue."

Alternatively, if the cultural metaphors are drawn from sport they can say a great deal about teamwork, or lack thereof? "The name of the game here is…." "I suggest we wait until the next inning." "We have got to pull together." "We took too many punches in the last round." Perhaps the language is more like that of the concerned father? "What's important here is our sense of family." Organizations where a sense of community is valued use language that enunciates that sense of unity. "Make sure everyone is on board." "We have to come together on this." The new executive who is attuned to the language is listening to nothing less than the very heartbeat of the organization. See also Chapter one for comments on language.

Beyond the metaphors, the new executive should be highly attentive to the stories that describe past events. Stories are likely to be a far more accurate characterization of events than anything that may have found its way into the company's literature. Leadership and story telling are synonymous. Stories that include the customer are particularly revealing. Moreover, stories divulge who the heroes were and how they became heroes (what the organization sees as heroic).

Humor is another important signpost. Any one who has ever worked in the North of England or in Australia cannot help but notice how central humor is to their way of working together. Often self-depreciating, pointed, and satirical, it can be either a unique means to build shared understanding or a weapon used to belittle and isolate; a means to magnify and inflame, or a way to draw a richness out of individual difference.

Pride is another key factor to observe. It is easy to recognize. Pride sets out in unambiguous terms the source of an individual's satisfaction. Even in small amounts it is infectious. Alternatively, the absence of pride is a silence that should be listened to. The new executive should be sensitive to opportunities, products, issues, events, and/or situations that draw out a sense of pride. Pride can be tapped, reveled in and built on. Conversely, injured pride, pride that is quashed, pushed back, diluted or held up to ridicule, leaves an employee resentful and holds them back from full participation and commitment.

Moving into a new role is like opening a book, reading slowly page by page, until the story unfolds. Except, instead of one book there are many. Much of the information, the whole story, lies not within the new organization alone but with customers, suppliers and others in alliance with the organization. In understanding the culture the new executive should make spending time with customers a high priority. There are things about the organization's culture that only the customer knows. Perhaps even more important is time spent with customers whose contracts and accounts have been lost.

Consultants, particularly the ones who work across the industrial/commercial sector, are similarly an invaluable source of insight. Their expertise is one thing, but, in addition to this, the orientation of the consultant him or herself can be telling. The behavior of the consultant, the style he or she adopts and his or her methodology reflect either well or poorly on the executive who hired him or her – an executive in a new role can determine what the hiring executive is worried or confident about through the kinds of consultants he or she has hired. In some cases, the consultant may represent the ideal that the hiring executive is striving to achieve.

In watching and listening, the new executive is building a sense of how things happen. Each meeting, each observation, each question answered represents an additional thread of understanding. When woven together, the executive in a new role has an accurate sense of the design and fabric of the organization. Now the executive is in a position to find some early answers to the following important questions: What seems to be important? What are the worst things that seem to go wrong? Where are the threats to the organization deemed to be? Is the business managed from the outside-in or the inside-out? Is it an "I" or a "we" culture? What dominates - organizational or personal values? Is this a place people seem to be at ease? How free do people seem to be to make decisions? What is the glue that seems to keep things together? How does information flow? What are people proud of? To what do people seem sensitive? Is it an organization where people feel free to criticize things that the organization has done? How is the criticism framed? Who is blamed? To whom are criticisms and complaints delivered? Is this an open or a hidden process (the committee or the water cooler)? Who is admired? Why? How do people seem to learn? Where does the power lie? Why?

Early insight into the new culture is a necessary step in the integration process. It is essential because it starts to provide answers to the critical question: Is how I got here aligned with future success?

The executive's orientation, background, and mind-set are his or her greatest strengths; they are why he or she is in the new role. But those same qualities represent the new executive's Achilles' heel, his or her greatest potential weaknesses. Failing to understand where past experience is out of synch with the needs of the new role is the single major reason why an executive moving into a new role fails.

Lack of attention to cultural fit is typically the biggest weakness in an organization's recruitment process. Without a robust understanding of the culture it is impossible to define the role effectively (see Chapter five). Moreover, it follows that without an in-depth understanding of the role it is all but impossible to meaningfully define the competencies that outline successful performance. There is, however, a deeper rooted problem: organizational culture is a subtle and ephemeral thing, spoken about in broad philosophical terms but not something with enough substance to have real meaning when it comes to day-to-day decisions.

Confusion over culture is hardly surprising; even the experts disagree. For business consultants, culture is about alignment drawn out of adherence to a set of shared values. Anthropologists look to symbolism, language, imagery and how people learn to describe differences between tribes or communities. A third line of thought stresses the importance of the role of leadership; the distribution of power and the members' freedom to act; the tactics used to resolve conflict; and the means by which tension between the formal and

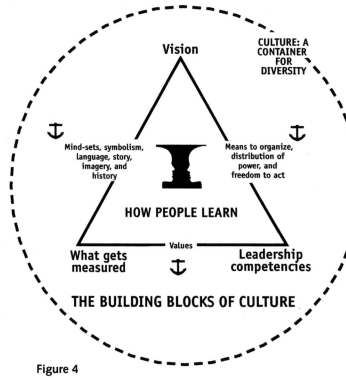

CULTURE: A CONTAINER FOR DIVERSITY

Vision

Mind-sets, symbolism, language, story, imagery, and history

Means to organize, distribution of power, and freedom to act

HOW PEOPLE LEARN

Values

What gets measured

Leadership competencies

THE BUILDING BLOCKS OF CULTURE

Figure 4

informal organization is acted out, as ways to draw back the cultural veil.

Something that is often overlooked when describing organizational change is that culture is never static. That is not to say that culture necessarily changes quickly – it took the Catholic Church three and a half centuries to admit that Galileo Galilei was right. Conversely, do nothing, and the culture will change. "Drift" is probably a better term. Without the tools to steer it effectively, the organization's culture is like an iceberg adrift in the South Atlantic – carried along, not with a destination in mind but subject to the whims of the strongest current.

When it comes to "steering" and aggressively changing the rate at which the culture changes, it can be argued that there are two quite distinct forces at play. The first can be captured under the term "cultural anchors," deeply embedded dimensions of the culture that unless addressed, unless dragged up from the bottom, are destined to frustrate any efforts to bring about change. The second are those elements of the culture that, once positioned effectively, move the culture in the direction needed. The first includes issues such as mind-sets, symbolism, language, imagery, the company's history, the means to organize, the way power is distributed, and the organization's values. Steerage comes from the vision, a determination regarding the nature and quality of the leadership needed and something that is often overlooked, that which is measured is that which is deemed important. Both threads are vital. Combined, when woven into a strong and durable fabric, they represent the warp and the weft of culture. **See Figure 4**. Scratch the surface of change initiatives that fail and it becomes quickly apparent that either the organization lacks the strength, courage and/or will to lift the cultural anchors, or alternatively, the leadership provided is devoid of the passion, authenticity and/or the emotional drive needed to build sustained commitment to the course being charted.

To make the integration process meaningful, the new executive has to get involved. And that means getting involved in defining, understanding, and adapting to the new culture.

Clearly, there are a number of ways to look at culture. For the savvy new executive, finding a way through this cultural maze begins with the organization's cultural anchors. With this in mind, what follows are three distinct but complementary ways for the new executive to better understand "how things happen around here": Culture as values; Culture as a means to organize and distribute power; and Culture as seen through the lens of mind-set, symbolism, language, story, imagery and history. A fourth dimension of cultural understanding, how people learn, serves to pull all of the threads of the cultural tapestry into a unifying weave.

Culture as values

The concept of organization culture is typically introduced through values. Deal and Kennedy (*Corporate Cultures*, pg. 21) argue that values "provide a sense of common direction for all employees and guidelines for their behavior. For all those who hold them, shared values define the fundamental character of the organization and the attitude that distinguishes it from others." Values, then, form "the heart of the corporate culture" (*Corporate Cultures*, pg. 14).

James Heskett and Leonard Schlesinger have also recognized the contribution of core values to cultural definition. In *The Leader of the Future*, they suggest that "at the heart of the new leadership is a rediscovery of the need to define, shape, and use the commonly held core values of the organization" (pg. 114). Put simply, values suggest the ways self-management and leadership can be distributed over the whole of the organization.

General Electric made a public statement that executives who don't live the values, regardless of their performance history, would not remain in their employ. Levi Strauss (many would say mistakenly) decided to turn its back on a major opportunity in China because Levi's leadership believed that to compete there successfully meant that it would have to compromise its values. Tylenol's swift response to product tampering was rooted in its belief, and in its courage, in acting out its values. A new executive joining those enterprises would ignore the organization's values at his or her peril.

Values are often included in the company's literature. It is not unusual to find an organization's values printed boldly and framed in the reception area. The problem: what the organization's literature says and how people actually behave are often out of alignment.

Values are what people do and not what they say. The executive in a new role needs to find out what the "real values" are. To do so, they would do well to ask the following questions of their organization: What happens when something goes wrong? If a customer complains who gets involved? Who gets promoted? What behavior is rewarded by the compensation system? What does the guy on the loading bay believe is important? What gets controlled from the corporate office and what doesn't? The last time things got tough what got cut and what didn't? Who counts for most, the shareholders or the "so called" stakeholders? What sort of information is needed to make an acquisition decision?

This notion of defined and reassuring values as a constant point of reference for all employees may seem ideal, but there is a downside. Take IBM, for instance: as early as the 1960's, IBM was known as an organization that managed through its values. Respect for the individual, in particular, was espoused as the key reason for IBM's phenomenal success. IBM is a good example of both the strength and the danger of values as a means to orchestrate culture. Values at IBM were a way to instill consistency and to ensure a sense of focus. IBM's customers in rural Kentucky or in New York all got the "best possible service." Their determination to adhere to defined values, however, resulted in a situation where even the uninitiated could spot an IBMer at thirty paces. They all looked the same, dressed the same, carried the same briefcase, spoke the same and, presumably, thought the same.

Through its values IBM had built a sturdy and durable bridge to its customer base. It was a bridge that could take a lot of traffic. Unfortunately, it was a bridge that only went to one location – fine if that's where the customer happens to be.

Unfortunately for IBM, many of their customers moved upstream. IBM's challenge thus became to build a new bridge, one that was portable, one that could be moved as their customers moved - a pontoon bridge. The problem: operating off an ever-changing platform demanded a high degree of comfort with ambiguity. The dilemma: those who felt constricted by IBM's rigidity, those comfortable with ambiguity, the very employees they now needed, were already upstream working for the competition.

The final dilemma concerning values surfaces when organizations attempt to define their values in Dallas and implement them with passion and **consistency** in Moscow, Karachi, New Delhi, and Santiago. Only a naïve expatriate would expect to find that integrity meant the same thing in his new role in Calcutta, India as it did in his previous position in Racine, Wisconsin.

Culture as means to organize and distribute power

The North American business media is quick to praise those who wear the mantle of leadership. When the honors are handed out to the "raiders," and "white knights," however, those made redundant by these champions of industry are lucky if they are mentioned as a footnote.

By comparison, when Volkswagen, the German auto manufacturer, decided it had to downsize its European workforce, it did so not by mass redundancy but by reducing the hours employees worked.

Microsoft is one of the success stories of this or, for that matter, any other era. Its aggressive growth, warrior-like tactics and ability to stay debt free makes it a favorite among high-tech investors. Moreover, Microsoft's young workforce seems to be more than willing to put up with living in what has been described as a pressure cooker.

The Shell Group operates by yet another modus operandi. Arie De Geus, one of those involved with creating and implementing scenario planning for Shell, said: "From the top of the Shell Group down there is no traditional mechanism to resolve conflict. The group has no CEO. The chairman of the managing directors is *primus inter pares*, first amongst peers" (*The Living Company*, pg. 191).

Brazil's Semco works to give employees a real stake in the company's performance. Ricardo Sempler, Semco's President, explains: "About a third of all Semco employees have the option of taking a pay cut of up to 25% and then receiving a supplement raising their compensation to 150% of normal if the company has a good year" (*Maverick*, pg. 333). Moreover, Semco has no organization chart, no titles, no secretaries, no receptionist, and employees set their own work hours.

The examples given describe different cultures, different ways for organizations to act. These differences are rooted in a range of factors but are primarily a blend of history, regional expectations, and the competitive environment – factors that become manifest in the way the business organizes, distributes power and extends freedom to act.

At first glance, the differences appear to be so significant as to suggest that every organization lives exclusively within its own space and time. If one steps back, however, common patterns emerge. One can identify four distinct domains that describe the range of alternative cultures, four distinct identities that point to their underlying cultures (1) Management by the Numbers; (2) Patron-Dominated; (3) Hunter-Gatherer; and (4) Community Based. **See Figure 5 and Figure 6.**

For many over the age of forty, the traditional Anglo-American model of capitalism has shaped their concept of a successful organization. It is, in essence, management by the numbers. Tightly controlled, most comfortable when competing on price, ever seeking to do what it has always done better, these organizations have become edifices of power to those who see size and ability to compete on cost as a measure of success. Long the realm of a commodity mind-set, these organizations are

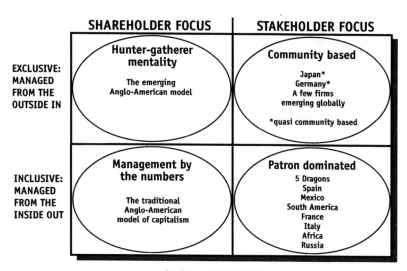

GLOBALISATION AND
THE CLASH OF CULTURES

Figure 5

	Management by the numbers	Patron-dominated	Hunter-gatherer	Community based
THEME	profitability	"father" knows best	shareholder value	quality of life for those involved
STRENGTHS	there is never any confusion as to who is in charge	speed of decision-making	always seeking new customers; new technology	innovation
LIMITATIONS	power resides with the few	"patron" is told only what he/she wants to hear	replacing a charismatic leader	high investment in learning
LEADERSHIP	when things not going well: slash and burn	ultimately rule by fear	entrepreneurial	in true communities self-regulating
LEARNING	yet one more cost	instruction	exploration	play
ACHILLES' HEEL	finding talent	promoting talent: succession	growing and keeping talent	rewarding talent
TEAM APPROACH	boxing	the opera	a pride of lions	NASA
GREATEST FEAR	a competitor who changes the value proposition	giving up control	the competitor over the horizon	a more compelling vision elsewhere
FREEDOM TO ACT	power over	power with: ask permission	power to	power from
BUSINESS MODEL	low cost producer	operational excellence	customer intimacy	be first and fail fast
DOMINANT MENTAL MODEL	the lone ranger	the family	the hunt	the village

Figure 6

anchored in a financially dominated, *power over*, mechanistic, hierarchical, centralized, leadership philosophy.

The origins of management by the numbers model lies with management pioneers such as Frederick Winslow Taylor, whose stop watch approach and passion for measurement, fueled an explosion of productivity that long outlived his death in 1915. If Taylorism provided a "scientific" formula for how much a worker could produce, Henry Ford provided, in the assembly line, the perfect manufacturing "machine."

Management by the numbers approach came to its full flowering in the 1960s with the birth of the conglomerate. The theme: with numbers you can manage anything. It reached its zenith with Harold Geneen of ITT whose belief in analysis was overshadowed only by the zeal for financial reengineering displayed by the asset strippers of the 1980s.

Lack of agility, a head and hand mentality, misuse of intellectual capital and inherent problems with employee loyalty has resulted in the gradual – although it still dominates some sectors - demise of the traditional Anglo-American model. In its place has sprung up a no less aggressive culture but one where hunting and gathering has replaced the lust for slow strangulation of the enemy. For management by the numbers organizations, short-term profitability rules supreme. For its successor, Economic Value Added (EVA) and the total wealth created for investors (Market Value Added) dominate. The success of Amazon.com is a case in point.

In the traditional model, value is created through "real assets" such as capital, plant, and equipment. In Hunter-Gatherer organizations value is created through knowledge creation, the power of people to innovate, and shared best practice. The former business model, in that it restricts power and access to information to the few, strongly militates against people thinking and working together. Management by the numbers organizations are, of necessity, *power over* cultures.

Hunter-Gatherer organizations are personified by the acquisitive, often cash rich, high-tech, fast moving enterprises that thrust their network of electronic tentacles outwards from Northern California. They are always on the lookout for new game or more fertile territory. Because their success is based on speed, aggression, quick thinking, and collaboration, they demand loyalty and discipline.

In their different ways, Bill Gates, Michael Eisner, the late Roberto Goizueta, and Larry Ellison all typify the Hunter-Gatherer passion for the chase. All enjoy displaying the trophies that tell others of their successes.

Not unlike their manage by the numbers ancestors, Hunter-Gatherer organizations have migrated far beyond their cultural home. As for values, these are organizations created, honed and shaped for and by the hunt not the hunters! The two icons of the Hunter-Gatherer domain: Steve Jobs, for gathering a harvest from two different orchards since picking his first Apple, and Bill Gates because he has simply out-hunted his contemporaries.

If Jobs and Gates share the entrepreneurial Hunter-Gatherer crown no one more personifies the corporate Hunter-Gatherer way than Jack Welch of General Electric. His legacy: leadership is about creating value, get out of businesses where there is no competitive advantage, push strategy down into the operations, throw out the policies and procedures, strip out unnecessary layers, share best practice, coach and then coach some more, and flood the place with feedback. As Welch so elegantly displays, a Hunter-Gatherer culture is predicated on a *power to* mentality.

There is a third dominant organization form, one that exists globally but one that has reached its most refined state in Latin cultures: Patron-dominated. It is also a business form that best describes the underlying culture of organizations operated out of the Asian Five Dragons. Run by one individual or one family, often with a steel fist inside a velvet glove, Patron organizations can be highly successful.

Here, loyalty to the Patron, and the Patron's values, dominates all other business considerations which, in turn, often results in market myopia and lack of openness. Because he or she dominates, Patron organizations lose much of their focus on values, energy and inspiration when the Patron dies. Fiat, the Irvings of Eastern Canada, and Mars are all examples of successful Patron organizations.

The two faces of the Patron organization can be seen in the form of Robert Maxwell, "the bouncing Czech," who misused his power to strip his company's pension fund of 400 million pounds sterling, and Gianni Agnelli, the patriarch of Fiat. Known affectionately as "L'Avvocato" (the lawyer), Agnelli, left a business at the time of his retirement in 1996 that was 14 times larger in sales, and infinitely more influential, than the one he inherited thirty years earlier.

Patron dominated organizations are consistent in two things: (1) succession is always a major issue and (2) the culture is *power with*. Empowerment and higher forms of employee involvement can flourish in a Patron dominated organization but only after those involved have sought and received permission.

The fourth domain is, for some organization design professionals, the suggested model for the next generation. The argument goes that executives, managers, and shop-floor workers alike are yearning for what can best be described as a sense of community. What is proposed is that organizations operating as a true community offer much that is missing from the organizational forms that have been the drivers of wealth in the Twentieth Century: a sense of belonging, caring, self-discipline, significance for all the stakeholders, true ownership, values that encompass individual needs, and a greater emphasis on social responsibility.

Community-based organizations are yet to fully flower but are coming to first stages of bloom in enterprises such as The Body Shop, parts of Shell, BHP's remote mine-site in

Cannington, Queensland, and Ricardo Semler's Semco. Organization as community is also expressing itself in a number of unique, self-organizing, collaborative ventures springing up on the Internet.

Many Japanese and German businesses, in that social responsibility underscores much of how they act, (or are allowed to act), are rooted in a strong sense of community (social values). Because true community emphasizes inclusion and self-regulation (as opposed to government controls) it would be more appropriate, however, to describe their overall business philosophy as "quasi community."

The healing process in South Africa and the leadership provided by Nelson Mandela are a constant source of inspiration for those who believe in the value of community as a business model for the Twenty-First Century.

Fueling the debate on community is what some economists call "natural capitalism." Their argument follows the view that if natural capital – forests, energy, water and so on – was accurately valued, there would be a dramatic reduction in resources use by the developed nations. An example of this is that the true cost of environmental damage, brought about by slash and burn farming, is not factored into the cost of a hamburger.

Those delivering the message of natural capitalism make two other points. The first is that the environment represents a tremendous business opportunity that few organizations have aggressively factored into their value creation model. The second is that to build commitment and release human potential, corporate values must be anchored in the needs of workers, the host communities and the customer (stakeholders). It is interesting to note that a UK study by Professor Duncan Gallie (*Restructuring the Employment Relationship,* 1998) established that only 8% of employees in the UK believe that their values and those espoused by the organization are similar. The message from those suggesting a role for natural capitalism: how the organization interacts with nature affords the leaders of tomorrow untold and, up to now, dramatically understated possibilities.

Perhaps the best known advocate of community as a way to organize is Anita Roddick, the founder of The Body Shop International. With 1,200 branches in 45 countries, Roddick is the UK's largest retailer. Using her stores to promote social activism, Roddick describes her mission "as service, as serving the weak and frail and bringing the concepts of social justice into the organization."

There is little evidence that the community styled organizations are going to quickly dethrone those following a Hunter-Gatherer path. If anything, the evidence suggests the contrary. The loss of lifetime employment in Japan and the ambivalence in Germany over the role of Government in the wealth creating process serve to expose the more apparent flaws in the stakeholder model. The problem: community-based organizations operate on a *power from* philosophy. The challenge: building consensus across widespread, *power from*, constituencies lies outside of the capability of the current generation of networking tools.

Culture as seen through the lens of mind-set, symbolism, language, story, imagery and history

Organizations shape the behavior of their workforce in a myriad of ways. The history of the firm, the language used, symbolism, imagery, and story all form the container that continuously echoes the cultural "voice." For successful organizations this "noise" is a means to replicate a healthy DNA. Conversely, if the enterprise is faced with a new competitive landscape, if the territory it is about to cross is alien, the established cultural building blocks both shape and limit what is possible.

This can be seen clearly as organizations go through different stages of ongoing growth (and decline). An apt metaphor for these stages of growth compares these platforms of transition to the changes of the seasons: preparing the ground, planting, growing, and harvesting. From a business standpoint, a fifth is probably needed: turnaround. Note: different parts of the organization are often at different stages of growth.

The executive in a new role should add as a lens of cultural awareness the "season" he or she finds him or herself in. Indeed, each season requires its own language, stories, symbolism, imagery, and, most important of all, mind-set. More precious than rubies is the executive who is a "man for **all** seasons."

The ability to manage turnaround is, in particular, a skill that seems to be reserved for a select few. Organizations seeking this sort of transformation will be gravely disappointed if they recruit someone for the role who does not have a track record of success in leading previous turnarounds. Not only do they put the organization at risk, but they are embarking on a tremendously expensive training program. Even for those with a successful track record, as the story of Al Dunlap clearly displays, what works at American Can, Lily Tulip, Crown Zellerbach, and Scott Paper Co. doesn't necessarily work at Sunbeam. After watching "Chainsaw" rip out half of the company's staff and 87% of its products, Sunbeam's investors were then able to watch their stock crash.

In practice, turnaround exponents tend to be a breed apart. For that reason, organizations are well advised, once the turnaround has largely been completed, to turn the business over to someone else.

The new executive must be acutely aware of the stage of business development he or she has inherited. Moving from a harvester role into a business start up (planter) demands not just new skills but a totally different leadership agenda. Similarly, transition from planter to grower means that the new executive must be sharply aware of (1) the language, symbolism, story and mind-set in place and (2) that needed for the team to succeed.

Culture as learning

Arguably the richest way to look at culture is to understand how people in the organization learn. How people learn, for example, dramatically impacts how they approach change. Do they wait for crises, and act in response? Do they strive to continuously grow or is personal development a purely defense mechanism? Do people see being at the edge as a business imperative or does the status quo rule?

Organizational learning is a much vaunted term, the bastion of rhetoric from many an organizational change "guru." Without an explanation of **how** people learn, however, it is a kite without a string; we can all admire the beauty of that thing flying above us, but we're in no way connected to it.

This story is about how people learn:

I was walking in the local park and happened to see something that from personal experience was quite new. A mother was teaching her young child how to ride a bicycle. What was interesting is that she had developed a very creative way to do so. Taped to the frame of the small bicycle and with its upswept blade protruding slightly above and a little behind the bicycle seat, was a sawn off hockey stick. The value of the hockey stick soon became apparent: on the straight-aways the mother could let the little guy have his head; on the curves, however, when he became a little unsure "mom" could reach in and provide support.

A little later I saw a different version of the same scenario only this time the story took the learning to a different plateau. A teenage boy was engaged in the most remarkable tricks on his specially constructed bicycle. Some of the flips and twists he clearly knew how to do; others he was attempting for the first time.

Walking home, I saw the more familiar model: a young father was teaching his daughter to ride her bicycle - a brand new little red machine supported by training wheels.

It was only later I realized that what I had seen was three quite distinct approaches to and levels of *learning*.

The child with the training wheels was **learning**. It was structured learning with little opportunity for experimentation. The child with the hockey stick was **learning how to learn** but where the physical surroundings provided limits or boundaries. The teenager was also **learning how to learn but whatever boundaries he came up against were entirely self-imposed**.

The experience exposed, simply and elegantly, three distinct plateaus of learning: simple learning; learning how to learn where the context is limited by the physical constraints; and learning how to learn where the individual's innovation and creativity represent the only limits.

I realized this was also exactly how children react to a new toy. At first, they play with the toy in much the same way as the toy's designer had anticipated. Within short order, however, a stage best described as exploration takes over. It is as if the child is thinking what will happen to the toy if....? Sooner or later, and often sooner, the toy is put away, broken or lost. The learning is not lost, however. It reappears in play, fantasy and imagination.

Is how I got here aligned with future success?

These three learning plateaus are a robust way to explain different organization forms (cultures). Described as three **Territories (T)** over which organizations chart their change journey, **Figure 7** outlines the underpinning assumptions that occur at each stage of learning. The new executive, whose skills and way to work have been developed and honed in a T1 environment and who, in moving to a T2 culture, attempts to reenact his/her old way to work, will fail. Equally poignant, he or she will in all probability have no idea why they are failing. The response: try harder. The outcome: harsher disconnects, exclusion, and isolation.

The new executive who has been hired because of his/her track record in initiating change should not be surprised if frustration sets in as a result of trying to achieve in a T1 business that which has worked so well in a T2 climate.

T2 organizations that get involved in takeovers and mergers should not be disappointed when the quality systems, process orientation, and approach to information technology that they value so highly are rejected by the T1 organization they just acquired. T1, T2 and T3 are not merely different ways to act they are, more to the point, different ways to think! They stem from different cultural models.

Similarly, the executive assuming leadership of the T3 corporate office in Florida should not be shocked to find that the performance management approach that works so well in Florida is an unmitigated disaster when introduced into the T1 subsidiary based in Paris.

T1 organizations are easy to identify. Hierarchical, boss driven, micro-managed, the "mechanism" by which things get done is fear. Fear of asking new questions, fear of stepping outside of the established

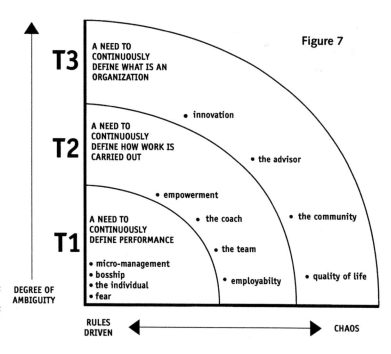

Figure 7

T3 — A NEED TO CONTINUOUSLY DEFINE WHAT IS AN ORGANIZATION

T2 — A NEED TO CONTINUOUSLY DEFINE HOW WORK IS CARRIED OUT

• innovation

• the advisor

• empowerment

T1 — A NEED TO CONTINUOUSLY DEFINE PERFORMANCE

• the coach

• the community

• the team

• micro-management
• bosship
• the individual
• fear

• employabilty

• quality of life

DEGREE OF AMBIGUITY

RULES DRIVEN ←——→ CHAOS

LEADERSHIP AND DISCONTINUOUS CHANGE

order, fear of making suggestions that could lead to redundancy. Much as we might like to think otherwise, the T1 organization still thrives. That having been said, T1 organizations in their pure form represent an extremely inefficient means to leverage human capital. The inevitable outcome: not a few organizations, even those still wedded to hierarchy and control, have evolved into what can best be described as "soft" T1 business models.

T2 organizations operate, think and flow entirely differently to their T1 counterparts. The team, rather than the individual, becomes the basic building block; process as a way to create value becomes the norm; decision-making moves as close to the customer as possible; traditional notions of supervision are cast aside; and organizational agility rules. Coaching is a natural extension of the management process within a T2 climate.

The traditional "manage by the numbers" organization is inevitably, and often irrevocably, T1. Although there are some notable exceptions, Patron organizations are likewise, more often than not T1. Operational excellence is invariably the value proposition pursued by T1 organizations. Hunter-Gatherer organizations, because of the need for responsiveness and agility, have to move to T2 to survive. A T2 culture allows the organization to offer customer intimacy as a way to compete.

T3 as an organizational form — organizations where innovation, ideas, and an ability to continuously realign resources with rapidly unfolding opportunities — has yet to become fully established. The distinguishing characteristic of a true T3 (virtual) organization is one where the value chain is exclusively digital. Using this definition, the "clicks and bricks" Internet success stories are not virtual organizations.

T3 organizations take three distinct forms: (1) temporary "virtual" organizations such as those that dominate the music and film industries; (2) organizations that are organized exclusively around projects where the outcome is knowledge creation e.g. a new organization in its immediate start-up phase or a research unit/group; and (3) pure virtual (T3) organizations. An excellent example of the latter is the development of the Linux operating system. Originally developed in 1991 by Linus Torvald when a computer-science student at the University of Helsinki, he decided that the best way to make his system "live" was by giving it away for free on the Internet. Since then thousands of interested users/programmers in all parts of the world have added to, modified and evolved the system to the point where today it represents one of Microsoft's most potent competitors. All this in an organization where there are no salaries, no one is in charge, there is no hierarchy and the only glue that keeps it together is community of interest.

People in T3 organizations, because of their own high investment in intellectual capital, are likely to be highly mobile. As a result, the glue that keeps a T3 organization together has to be an extension of the needs of those who make up the organization: a sense of community and a high quality of life.

And where do values fit in? T1 organizations are focused and project values skewed towards the organization's needs. "We sell cheaper," says nothing about the needs of the employees. T2 organizations, on the other hand, invariably attempt to strike a balance between the needs of the shareholders and the needs of the other stakeholders. A number of T2 organizations even go so far as to list both company and employee values. In T3 organizations, ownership and employment is indistinguishable and, because the employees are the company, the personal values they espouse are those that guide behavior.

This does not mean that the organization will, of necessity, be exclusively T1, T2 or even T3. Although tending to be dominated by one form, the likelihood is that the organization will straddle two or even all three of the learning platforms identified. In many instances the same employee will work concurrently in more than one culture. An organization such as Toyota is a good example. A job on the line, even where the work involves job rotation and encompasses issues such as quality, is still a (soft) T1 culture. In working on a process team to drive cost out of the process the same employee, however, is moving into a T2 culture. This need to work in two, or even a range of different cultures, at the same time is becoming the new business reality. The implications for teamwork, cross company synergy, problem solving, knowledge management and consensus building even for the established executive cannot be understated. For the new executive it's a world that demands that culture and all of the trailing implications must be understood.

The executive in a new role must step back and explore the kind of learning environment he or she has entered. The reality: moving from a T1 to T2/T3 environment represents far more than a change of role, it demands nothing less than a new way to think.

For the new executive, understanding the cultural domain he/she is entering is essential. It is an imperative because each of the organization forms outlined has a different way to act, a different personality, a different way for things to get accomplished and a different power nexus that has to be understood. Taking on a business turnaround without understanding what is implied is a short cut to disaster. The executive who elects to leave the safety of the London office where the notion of leadership is financial control and who, in moving into the Mexican subsidiary, expects to succeed by accessing the same mind-set is destined to fail.

Crossing cultural domains can be perilous and demands interpretative skill. The executive in a new role might find him or herself in a very new culture where the same words mean very different things and where the same problem has a very different solution. Moving to a Patron-dominated organization without expending effort to understand how to manage upwards will likely make for a short stay. And no one should even think about a move to Oracle or one of its Hunter-Gatherer competitors unless he or she is equipped mentally, physically and emotionally to run down the prey, fight off the wolves and eat the kill.

The executive in a new role should be keenly aware of the experience (as skill and baggage) he or she brings. He or she should also, in equal proportion, be sensitive to issues of fit, relevance, and the need to reach out and ask for help.

The cultural anchors, plus how people learn, have been presented as valuable ways to view culture. In essence, they are no more than different prisms through which the executive in a new role can start to answer the simple question: Is how I got here aligned with future success?

Chapter Two

Critical Learning

- Finding your way into the new role will require a careful reading of all of the "clues."

- The outward appearance of people, the use of space, color, symbolism, and artifacts, all represent invaluable ways to learn about the new environment.

- Language, and especially metaphor, is as valuable to the new executive as fingerprints are to the forensic expert.

- Culture can be defined in several ways. Three approaches, in particular, should be uppermost in the mind of an executive moving into a new role: (1) Culture as values; (2) Culture as a means to distribute power; (3) Culture as seen through mind-set, symbolism, language, story, imagery and history. A fourth, how people learn, serves to pull all the threads of the cultural tapestry into a unifying weave

---

Consequences

Culture is nothing less than a means to describe what success and failure looks like. If the new executive lacks the tools to explore and understand the new culture, he/she is trapped into assuming that what worked in the past is relevant and meaningful in the new situation.

Step back and reflect on the ideas that surfaced and the learning you take from this chapter. Consider the path you are on, the need to build relationships (fit), and your understanding of success in the new role (expectations). Think about what you need to stop doing, start doing, and that which you need to do differently.

What sort of team is this?

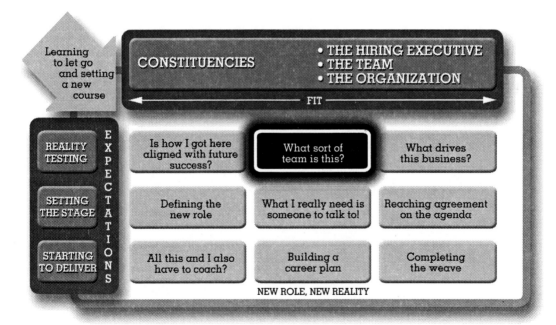

CONSTITUENCIES
- **THE HIRING EXECUTIVE**
- **THE TEAM**
- **THE ORGANIZATION**

FIT

Learning to let go and setting a new course

EXPECTATIONS			
REALITY TESTING	Is how I got here aligned with future success?	What sort of team is this?	What drives this business?
SETTING THE STAGE	Defining the new role	What I really need is someone to talk to!	Reaching agreement on the agenda
STARTING TO DELIVER	All this and I also have to coach?	Building a career plan	Completing the weave

NEW ROLE, NEW REALITY

What sort of team is this?

If the eyes can be said to be the window of the soul the team is the window that reveals the very spirit of the organization. The Italian poet Luciano de Crescenzo expressed this need for collaboration when he wrote: "We are all angels with only one wing. We can only fly by embracing each other."

Even before the promoted or parachuted executive arrives, the team will have discussed him or her. Informed input, scuttlebutt, innuendo and rumor will have created an opinion - good or bad. If the team has played a key role in the interview process, much of the anxious and territorial concern might already have found a voice.

For the incoming executive, starting to understand the new team, and the nature of teamwork in the organization in general, are important building blocks in the integration process.

Team building starts - whether undertaken purposefully or not - on day one. The first opportunity to interact, the first meeting, the first presentation start to set a tone and communicate the new executive's beliefs about teamwork. You might be trying to get a read on them, but you need to be aware that they are trying equally hard to get a read on you. As a result, the new executive should not wait until deep into the integration process before asking him or herself key questions concerning his or her teams. Questions like, "What sort of team is this?" "What sort of team am I going to need?" "What and how can I make a contribution to the team(s) I have now joined?"

Some executives new to their role hold back when it comes to developing team spirit. Their experience, their personal orientation, is that teamwork looks good as a topic on the shelves of management bookstores, but it takes a bunch of hard working and tough minded **individuals** to get things done. But going it alone is the very worst thing that a new executive can do. Not everyone in the organization will be rooting for the new guy's success.

Some, and even some on the new team, will personally feel a little more secure if the new person starts to struggle. If the executive in a new role reinforces this opposition by conveying a spirit of detachment, a sense of "I don't really need you guys," he or she will be sowing the seeds of their own downfall.

It is also worth bearing in mind that the executive in a new role has joined not one but many different teams and to succeed, will have to perform a number of different team roles. What follows are concepts, concerns, and connections that must be part of the new executive's thinking as he or she meets with and develops within his or her new team(s).

A team is not a team is not a team

Most executives moving into a new role and onto a new team generally think their task is simply to improve the way "my people" work together. What typically is not explored are the multiple possibilities open to the team. For example, the term "team" is a very imprecise way to define a wide range of potential ways for groups to operate in unison. The dilemma: unless the new executive understands what sort of team he or she is trying to create, unless the way the team comes together is aligned with the business purpose, the result is likely to be wasted effort and confusion. Moreover, it should be always be borne in mind that there is only one thing worse than a poor team - a great team going in the wrong direction!

Two factors shape what sort of team is needed: (1) the degree of integration needed between the different business units; (2) the organization's relationship with its customer base. When considering potential

Figure 8	**PRODUCT DRIVEN:** The relationship with the customer based, for the most part, on price, quality, and availabilty	**CUSTOMER DRIVEN:** The product/service either reengineered or built to the customer's specifications	**MARKET DRIVEN:** The product or service developed in anticipation of the customers' and potential customers' emerging needs
Potential value creation as a result of synergy between business units and/or companies, low.	**SKEET SHOOTERS** distinguished by INDEPENDENCE A RESULTS FOCUS SINGLE MINDEDNESS A PROPENSITY TO SHOOT DOWN SOMEONE ELSE'S BIRD	**THE AMERICAN FOOTBALL SQUAD** distinguished by TOUGH MINDEDNESS REPERTOIRE OF PLAYS WILLINGNESS TO CREATE HOLES FOR ITS STAR PLAYERS FIXED ROLES	**THE PIT CREW** distinguished by COMPETITIVENESS A DESIRE TO SERVE SPEED OF RESPONSE ABILITY TO ANTICPATE PROBLEMS INTER-TEAM RIVALRY
Potential value creation as a result of synergy between business units and/or companies, high.	**ROWING EIGHT** distinguished by DEPENDENCY COHESIVENESS BALANCE NEED FOR A SMOOTH COURSE	**THE SOCCER TEAM** distinguished by SYNERGISTIC FLOW INVOLVEMENT OF THE WHOLE TEAM ABILITY TO REDEFINE ROLES STAR PLAYERS ALSO HAVE TO BE TEAM PLAYERS	**12 METER YACHT CREW** distinguished by INTERDEPENDENCE A WILLINGNESS TO TAKE RISK LEARNING AT THE EDGE CAPACITY TO CHANGE DIRECTION COMFORT WITH AMBIGUITY

ALIGNING TEAM APPROACH WITH BUSINESS REALITY

team behavior, there are at least **six** variations of team organization. **See Figure 8.**

Skeet shooters: a knock 'em down, shoot 'em up group of individuals – tackles problems aggressively and pushes product (hard). A skeet-shooting team is interested only in the targets that come into their personal sights. They are measured purely in terms of their own score, and they understand that the one who blows apart the most targets is the winner. Skeet shooters can be highly effective where the relationship with the customer is product driven, and where creating synergy between the separate functional and/or operational parts is not really the primary goal.

Skeet-shooting teams are quick on the trigger – that is their virtue. So, don't expect that such a team is going to give up its successful ways easily and all of a sudden value shared learning and close customer relations.

The value added by skeet shooters is that they are self-contained, aggressive, and results driven. Their major limitation is that they get so used to knocking down ideas, problems and challenges, that they are prone to taking pot shots at other team members' "targets."

The rowing eight: a cohesive team, working together as one, with defined roles that are carried out with precision. A rowing eight comes together only where the members are carefully chosen and where there is an established balance within the team. In situations where the purpose is clearly established, where the course is marked, and where there is no debris in the water, the rowing eight will make great time - and look terrific while doing so. If conditions become rough, however, then the rowing eight is liable to capsize.

The lesson for those working with teams: the group may look good and it may be making great time, but, if it is not equipped to deal with upcoming white water, the team is unlikely to fit with a business context that is essentially customer driven.

Conversely, if the business is built around a great product, if the environment is in a steady state, speed and coordination may be more valuable than depth and stability.

The American Football team: tough and well trained, the Football team has a wide repertoire of plays that can be sent in to meet changing conditions and expectations. Built around very strict roles and rehearsed moves, the Football team is particularly good at creating holes for its star players to run through. The very best teams even make room for the quarterback to scramble (improvise) if something unexpected happens.

The constraint of the Football team is that it limits decision-making to one or two people in leadership roles. The Football-team formation also leaves little or no room for role mobility and so it is most successful where the pattern of plays is predictable and where everyone on the team sticks to set task(s).

The Soccer team: a soccer team carries many of the response capabilities of the American Football team while, at the same time, building teamwork around much more fluid and flexible patterns of play. Equally important, new plays can emerge naturally to fit the circumstances. There is ongoing participation of **all** of the players and sheer size has little impact on success. And, although roles such as the goalkeeper are constrained, the majority of team members get to play both offense and defense.

Because of its movement and flow, Soccer has developed the capacity to cross cultural boundaries, meaning that members from different backgrounds can play successfully together with an elegance that is quickly apparent. Because of this, the ensuing opportunity for shared learning - often on the international stage - can be extremely high. The tricky part of the soccer team is that, when the stakes are high, the team tends to avoid risk and reverts to patterns of interaction that simply protect themselves from being "scored against."

The pit crew: two things define the successful pit crew: speed of action, and the ability of the team to be prepared for the unforeseen. Pit crews are great at reading the conditions and can be extremely adaptive — they can actually turn problems into advantages. The pit crew, while characterized by frantic action, is equipped with a wealth of research and technical innovation. It is also a team with one overriding purpose: to serve.

The pit crew is, nevertheless, an instrument of competitiveness. It succeeds, or fails, based on its ability to move faster than the next team. The pit team is thus an ideal model where technical innovation, speed of action and superb team play are essential. If synergy between teams is demanded, however, a different team model needs to be explored.

The 12 meter yacht crew: a finely honed yacht crew is the master of its domain with a capacity to change direction, take advantage of the prevailing wind and use the forces pushing against it to distinct advantage. Flexibility of roles, an ability to respond to the unexpected and a willingness to push to the very edge are essential ingredients of the successful yacht crew.

Competing boats trying to usurp each other's wind will display a competitive spirit as keen as anything in sport. But if one of them makes a serious mistake and a life-threatening situation arises, then competition is typically pushed aside and the team will display a sense of genuine caring as they convert to rescue tactics.

* * * * *

The executive moving into new team situations needs to keep the Titanic in mind; what he or she sees on the surface may not be a good indication of what lies beneath, and a poorly navigated meeting will sink even the soundest vessel. Use caution when making assumptions about what sort of team you find yourself with. Moreover, keep in mind the kind of team you need to be successful – this determination can be made by taking into account the need for inter-team synergy and the organization's emerging relationship with its future customer base.

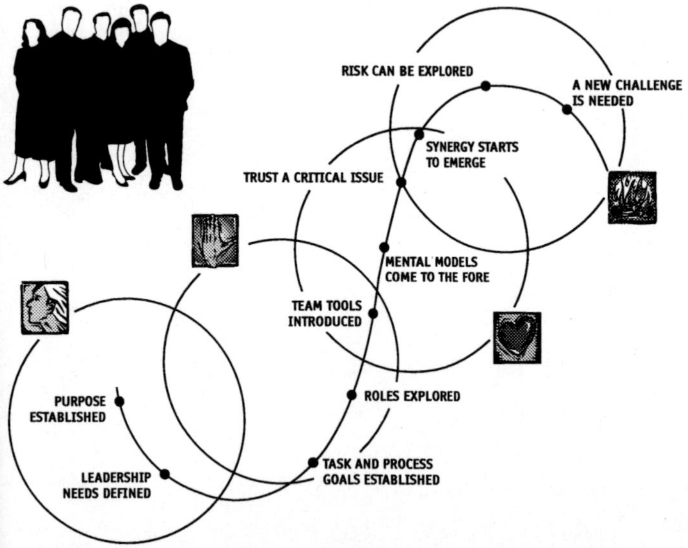

High performance teams don't just happen

Though it sometimes looks that way, successful teams do not grow in a random fashion. Effective teams evolve by developing skills and insights that enable them to transcend a series of critical developmental stages. **See Figure 9.**

Each stage, in turn, is comprised of a series of interactive challenges - process

RISK CAN BE EXPLORED

A NEW CHALLENGE IS NEEDED

SYNERGY STARTS TO EMERGE

TRUST A CRITICAL ISSUE

MENTAL MODELS COME TO THE FORE

TEAM TOOLS INTRODUCED

ROLES EXPLORED

PURPOSE ESTABLISHED

LEADERSHIP NEEDS DEFINED

TASK AND PROCESS GOALS ESTABLISHED

Figure 9   **THE 10 STAGES OF TEAM DEVELOPMENT**

problems that the team has to work through if it is to move to a point of maturity. As he or she looks at the new team and builds early insights about how the team should move forward, the new executive should be acutely aware of the stage of team development for **each** of the teams he/she is a member of. The stages themselves unfold in the following manner.

Raison d'être: the team needs to know why it was formed, its reason for being, its purpose, its broad mission. Without this elemental first step the team has no shape, no sense of direction and little upon which to build shared meaning. A new person on the team can be of immense service to the other team members by asking the simple question: "Why **are** we here?"

Leadership needs have to be defined: leaderless teams are a fantasy of well-meaning trainers with little hands-on experience. A team without leadership is like a ship without a rudder. A team without leadership is one devoid of a vibrant and empowering vision. And, like a ship, it may appear to make headway during calm weather, but the real test is the unforeseen problem, the unique event, the unanticipated storm that hits with full fury.

This does not mean that the leadership has to reside in a single individual. If there is a high parity of power between team members, if the environment is complex and the requirements are speed of response, the team will need a highly flexible approach to leadership.

Central to the role of team leadership *is building agreement regarding the team's values:* values define what has primacy, what is essential as opposed to what is merely important. The team's values provide the outer boundaries to self-management and initiative. The team's values are the basis of consistency, the wellspring of commitment and the source of team character. Without agreement and ongoing dialogue around the team's values, team leadership will remain rooted in the formal hierarchy. And, in such instances, a good deal of creative tension gets lost to emotional conflict with the eventual result that members "play it safe."

Establishing both task and process criteria: teams invariably excel at defining tangible task outputs – bottom line deliverables. But unless these are balanced by softer process outputs, the team's ability to develop is severely handicapped. Unless the team defines, in specific terms, **how** they want to work together, there is little the team can go on to evaluate their success as a team.

Team roles understood: teams, as opposed to individual output, create value because problems and opportunities are subject to a richer and more productive level of solution. But this does not mean that within a team different members cannot have different roles. Leadership is obviously one of the critical roles. Other roles are a product of the challenge on hand but to name a few, the team early on might designate a facilitator, a reporter, subject experts, an idea gatekeeper, process advisor, a team coach, idea generator, and someone whose role it is to challenge the group's mind-set.

Team tools utilized: over the years the topic of teamwork has been the subject of intensive, and wide-ranging research. A by-product of this work has been what amounts to a virtual avalanche of tools, diagnostic instruments, questionnaires, and team-focused processes.

Typical team tools include such things as problem solving models, personality inventories, leadership diagnostic instruments, team effectiveness questionnaires, multiple-input feedback techniques, facilitation training, the use of information technology as an adjunct to decision-making, process reengineering, TQM, and a host of others.

Improving team effectiveness through the introduction of meaningful team tools is like much else in life - essentially a matter of informed choice combined with good timing. A helpful early insight for the executive on a new team (or playing a new role on an old team) is to identify what tools the team uses.

However, let there be a word of warning here for the new executive: team tools can be slippery companions and what might be, in one situation, an excellent problem-solving method can in another be the basis of unnecessary conflict.

Bringing mind-sets to the surface: no one perceives reality – instead, we see the world around us through a set of filters. These filters are products of our upbringing, our history of success and/or failure, past experience, values, beliefs and our sense of personal identity. These filters allow us to make intuitive decisions; they are the basis of much of our judgment, and they allow us to process and make sense of a world that is becoming ever more complex. What this means is that each of us possesses a unique way of viewing the world, and a unique set of assumptions that determine how each of us defines success.

Exploring and bringing these individual differences to the surface is an important task for the team. If managed with sensitivity and candor, what could otherwise be a source of ongoing friction and unresolved conflict can become the basis of a creative and innovative approach to team issues. Like mines floating just below the surface in busy waterways, conflicting mind-sets will eventually sink even the most agile team. Brought to the surface, that same explosive mixture can be harnessed and added to the arsenal of the perceptive captain. These differing mind-sets can in fact form the basis of a level of creative tension that enhances the chemistry and internal dynamics of a high performance team.

Trust becomes a critical issue: trust may or may not be part of the dynamics of the team at early stages of development. Without the emergence of trust however, the team can never fully realize the collaborating stage of team development.

Trust surfaces in a number of ways. Team members begin to feel more comfortable in sharing their feelings, and so issues that team members would have, at an earlier stage of team development, let slide, now become the subject for respectful confrontation. With developed trust, when team members say they will do something, there is the assumption that it will be carried out. And trust means that conflict and individual difference can be a source of new insight and innovation rather than, as is the case in teams where there is little trust, ego-based defensive tactics.

Synergy starts to emerge: sadly, few teams reach this stage of maturity and, as a result, few teams reach their potential for breakthrough thinking. Teams that have leadership, that define the roles in a meaningful way, that have the courage to confront conflicting mind-sets and in so doing establish a climate of trust, start to see old challenges in an entirely new way. When synergy starts to emerge, when the whole becomes greater than the sum of the parts, when the creative juices start to flow, teams reap rewards out of the very differences that in other circumstances would have kept them apart.

A great deal has been written over the past three decades about the whole notion of synergy. Indeed, the Japanese have been, for a generation, praised as having the capacity to deliver on their planning strategies because the agreements themselves were drawn out of consensus rooted in team synergy. Because everyone on the team has their say, because all of the interested parties have an opportunity to put their finger prints on the decision, the implementation has the emotional support of **all** of those needed to carry it through.

What is missing from the mental architecture of most teams is the belief that team synergy can also be a factor in making faster decisions. One of the dilemmas with decision-making in immature teams is that by the time a decision has been made, the cutting edge of the opportunity has often been lost. By comparison, a team that develops a high level of trust and is comfortable with risk can, by moving to an intuitive, rapid fire, experience-based approach, transform its speed of decision-making.

Risk explored: with a higher level of trust comes a willingness on the part of the team to explore risk. Risk can take many forms. It might include confrontation with team members who have had difficulty buying into a team ethos – where there is no trust, such situations often lead to the fragmentation of the team. Exploring risk can also include addressing problems of inter-team rivalry, exploring new markets, revisiting lost customers, and challenging established systems and processes in the wider organization. If successful within "at risk" situations, the bonding between team members is dramatically heightened.

New challenge needed: a mature team, one that starts to consolidate all of the qualities and competencies described, is a little like a person with a sports car - no matter what the "law" says, he or she is going to want to push it to the limit. Teams that reach the level of maturity described start to lose energy unless the level and challenge of the work they face is aligned with the team's newfound capability.

When faced with a new challenge, one that stretches the team's resources and capabilities, there is an overriding need for the team to explore new ways for leadership to emerge. The team members will need to revisit many of the characteristics of behavior that previously made it successful.

As teams develop and as the inherent capability within the team surfaces, the team moves through four stages of growth: head, hand, heart and spirit.

Although there are some exceptions, such as high performance Operating Room teams, traditional boss-dominated groups rarely progress beyond the head and hand stages of group interaction.

To move to the higher levels of team maturity, the executive in a new role must cultivate within the team a degree of openness and a comfort with ambiguity. Both are the product, in large measure, of a participatory approach to decision-making.

So called self-managing teams need a lot of tender loving care

The business literature often trumpets the value of so called "self-managing" teams. Such teams are deemed self-managing because the tasks traditionally carried out by supervision have been collapsed into the work practices of the team. Examples of these practices include: scheduling; allocating work assignments; extended decision-making regarding issues such as quality and maintenance; process control; means to reduce working capital; performance measurement; recruitment of new team members; and even such taboo areas as employee discipline. Evidence suggests that to make self-managing teams a reality, a number of conditions have to be met:

- The team must be organized around a discrete arena of work – that is, an autonomous flow of activity that, **when viewed from the customer's perspective**, creates value for the customer (process). A move to a process focus makes redundant not only the traditional functional organization model but long held assumptions about management as an activity.

- Self-managed teams must be multi-skilled.

- The concept of whole jobs must be actively practiced - which means that job redesign is an active and aggressive means to align capability and opportunity.

- Success must be measured by feedback from customers.

- Process analysis, process redundancy, process redesign and, where appropriate, process innovation must be part of the way the team operates.

- Issues such as quality, and the ordering of non-capital items (e.g., hand tools) must rest with the team.

- The team must be skilled in simple industrial engineering skills (e.g., work measurement, or process mapping)

- The team must regularly meet with its customer(s).

- The performance management system should reward team performance, defined by one or more dimensions of increased value creation.

- Where the acquisition of new skills is part of the reward system, team members must play a role in the evaluation and endorsement of those new skills.

HITTING THE WALL → TALK HAS TO BE TRANSLATED INTO ACTION

Stages of growth / Constituency	Letting go of a command and control mind-set **MOVING AWAY FROM BOSSHIP**	Starting to form teams	Transition into team-based organization	Evolving as a team-based organization	Mature team-based organization
			LEARNING TO WORK AS A TEAM		
INDIVIDUAL	What's in it for me? Concerns about job security.	Balancing teamwork with agreed personal objectives overwhelms some team members.	Traditional notion of a job gives way to contribution defined through roles. Decision-making pushed closer to customers.	An emphasis on learning emerges. Ownership in many different forms becomes a focus. Those uncomfortable with level of ambiguity needed bail out.	Personal growth not restricted to the workplace. Some family issues can emerge. A holistic appreciation of quality of life becomes an issue.
TEAM	Both interested in, and threatened by the prospect of working differently.	Traditional command and control supervisor starts to become very uncomfortable with the degree of ambiguity demanded.	Experimenting leads to early understanding of team process. Guidance for the process owner essential.	Leadership emerges. Multi-skilling becomes the norm. Redundant process elements identified.	The teams need new challenges. Access to market place and source of best practice essential. Ongoing learning an imperative.
UPPER MANAGEMENT	Give directions. Uncomfortable in giving up power. Invariably, represent poor role models. Building a customer(s) value model essential.	The resources needed to support a process way of working creates shockwaves. Commitment to a process focus essential.	An understanding of value chain management starts to emerge. Functional managers start to deal with their role as competency coach.	Innovation emphasized in many different forms. Boundary between the company and its customers/suppliers stripped away.	Competing on value starts to embrace all of those in the value chain including the customer's customer and supplier's supplier.
REST OF THE ORGANIZATION	Cynicism focuses on the difficulty of making a process organization work. Who else has done this?	An understanding that changing the way the organization operates involves everyone. Some functional managers will want to pull back.	Alignment of all the elements of value creation come to the fore. Dramatic shift in relationship with key customers and major suppliers.	Maintaining the link between process way of working and overall business performance measures essential.	Share best practices. Overall organization performance must move beyond financial measures e.g. intellectual capital.
KEY ISSUES	Alignment with the organization's strategic drivers. The nature of dialogue between key stakeholders. Leadership.	Quality of training. Language used to describe the journey. Process focus. Selection of process owners.	Disassembling the established hierarchy. Building robust leadership models. 360° feedback. Customer, supplier alignment.	Organization structure, information technology, performance management, and the quality of human resource support dominate.	The process organization as a way to compete must dominate how everyone thinks.

Figure 10

- Mechanisms must be in place to allow information to flow across the organization. Such channels give team members instant access to not only critical customer and supplier information but information on the status of the other processes in the overall system.

- In organizations where unions are involved, the work and team processes created by the team must be monitored by a joint management-union steering committee.

- The role of the hierarchical manager must be replaced by that of coach and/or process owner.

Moving to self-managing teams is only possible if those responsible for creating and nurturing them have vision, patience, sensitivity and an ability to rise above the day-to-day. And the team process must be framed within the broader organizational context. The creation of such teams also demands an insightful understanding of the different plateaus of growth, a capacity to manage often conflicting constituencies, and the organizational craft to identify key issues at different stages of self-managing team evolution. **See Figure 10.**

Much of what is referred to as teambuilding only adds to the problem

The executive newly joining a team might think this is the perfect time to reach out for help – to engage in some teambuilding exercises. There will be no shortage of people offering to be the guide. Indeed, precious few major consulting houses fail to offer "solutions to team problems." For the most part, teambuilding interventions follow one of four directions:

(1) A consultant sits with the team as they face day-to-day operational challenges. The consultant's role is to provide honest feedback about the behavioral dynamics being played out, and to facilitate a shared understanding concerning what the team should focus on as they move forward.

(2) A series of personal and confidential interviews with each team member, followed by a teambuilding session where a summary of the information is fed back to team members. Led by a skilled facilitator, the feedback is presented as an emotional platform for self-examination, and the basis for improved team behavior.

(3) The team builds a competency model that describes the behaviors best aligned with

individual and team success. Multiple sources of feedback (including non-team members) are orchestrated by the use of 360° input. A teambuilding workshop uses the range of input to frame dialogue such that team members share their strengths and areas for improvement. The output of the session is an individual action plan complemented by "permission" amongst team members to coach each other on specific action items.

(4) The team is taken away from the every day and presented with an environment that breaks the pattern of ongoing work experience. Outward Bound can be such an experience, as can the raft trip, the ropes exercise, tap dancing, ballooning, drag cars, and a host of other experiences. The Russian military even offers the use of a Mig fighter for those teams willing to take the risk.

The idea behind this teambuilding approach is that the new environment provides a catalyst for the kinds of openness and self-discovery that are virtually impossible to create within the day-to-day context.

The "event" works best when framed as a metaphor for the opportunities and difficulties faced by the team. For this reason the outdoor activity or special activity must be designed/created specifically to meet the learning needs of the group. Learning is a mixture of exploration and play, and is both stimulating and enjoyable. Indeed many of those who had attended such sessions suggested their team had undergone (at least for the short term) a metamorphosis.

In some senses, the approach a given organization adopts is likely to be a function of the consultants they happen to meet. No doubt all, or any, of the processes outlined have high potential value. But the executive new to a team should be cautious because promise is not always the same as the delivery.

- Teambuilding interventions that fail to address broader systemic issues such as structure, information flow, the broader business context, the power of language, and/or the performance management approach, are destined to have little substantive impact.
- Teambuilding processes that don't include a robust way to describe culture (this is especially true when the team involved plays an international role) are flawed before they get under way.

- Teambuilding actions that don't pose tough questions about the team's leadership needs are likely to perpetuate rather than resolve dysfunctional behavior.

- Teambuilding approaches that start from an assumption that the team is broken and thus has to be fixed are likely to only find negative information. The assumption will create resentment, resistance, and the negative imagery that will accompany such approaches will likely perpetuate rather than resolve any dysfunctional team behavior. Breakthrough research in sports psychology strongly emphasizes the need for a coach to focus on the positive.

- Team development that is not built around a well thought through model of team development (see **high performance teams don't just happen**) is unlikely to be able to ground the event in a **meaningful** analysis of the team's needs.

But hey, don't throw the baby out with the bath water. Many of the processes described, if aligned with a healthy understanding of the broader market and cultural context, have true merit. For the executive new to a team, it is a matter of "buyer beware."

*   *   *   *   *

This chapter has covered several themes germane to successfully moving into a new team. Central to those is the need for the new executive to understand what sort of team he/she needs to create. It is also essential that the new executive understand the building blocks that go into the making of a great team. More and more organizations are attempting to build an environment where self-managed teams thrive. Delivery, however, is not the same as intent and the new executive should understand what it takes to make a self-managed team a working reality. Finally, if teambuilding is suggested, the new executive needs to know what is likely to work and what is not.

Those who know how to work through and with the new team make their own integration process infinitely easier. Locked up within the team is 90% of the knowledge and 95% of the "know-how" the executive in a new role needs to engineer fit. Don't forget - attempting flight with only one wing is likely to be both painful and frustrating.

Chapter Three

Critical Learning

- The new executive is joining many different teams.

- Teambuilding starts on day one.

- The new executive needs to understand the type of team the situation demands.

- High performance teams don't just happen – there are a series of critical learning steps that the team goes through.

- So-called self-managing teams need a lot of tender loving care.

- Much of what is described as "teambuilding" only adds to the problem.

Consequences

In a complex world, business is a team game. No executive – no matter how talented – can make it with a poor or inadequate team supporting him or her. In a world where speed is an imperative, the new executive needs to come to terms with the nature and needs of the team as soon as possible. Failure to do so, and/or lack of expertise in how to do so will inevitably result in early derailment.

Step back and reflect on the ideas that surfaced and the learning you take from this chapter. Consider the path you are on, the need to build relationships (fit), and your understanding of success in the new role (expectations). Think about what you need to stop doing, start doing, and that which you need to do differently.

_____

_____

_____

_____

_____

_____

_____

_____

_____

_____

_____

What drives this business?

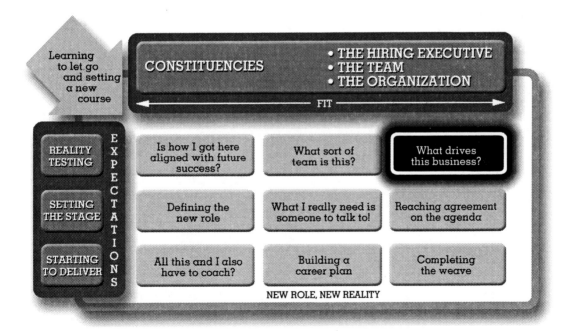

Learning to let go and setting a new course

CONSTITUENCIES
• THE HIRING EXECUTIVE
• THE TEAM
• THE ORGANIZATION

FIT

	EXPECTATIONS			
REALITY TESTING		Is how I got here aligned with future success?	What sort of team is this?	What drives this business?
SETTING THE STAGE		Defining the new role	What I really need is someone to talk to!	Reaching agreement on the agenda
STARTING TO DELIVER		All this and I also have to coach?	Building a career plan	Completing the weave

NEW ROLE, NEW REALITY

What drives this business?

In the mid 1930s, American anthropologist Lauriston Sharp lived for thirteen months with the Yir Yaront group of aboriginals, whose ancestral home lay at the mouth of the Coleman River on the west coast of Cork York Peninsula. Sharp found that the polished stone axes, which had been a feature of the band's life since ancient times, were rapidly being replaced by steel axes. Distributed by well-meaning missionaries, the steel axes proved not to make life easier, as the givers had intended, but they did much to destroy a way of life that was as old as man himself.

What Sharp discovered was that the stone axe played a very central role in the band's interpersonal, cultural, trading, social and kinship relationships. The stone for the axes could only be found several hundred miles away, and securing the materials was the basis of inter-group trading. The axes could only be "owned" by the male members of the group, and the women's need to borrow an axe constantly reinforced the male/female gender hierarchy. Making the axes was a skill held by the older members of the group, and their production was central to inculcating respect for the elders.

Because of the steel axes, "ownership became less well-defined, with the result that stealing and trespassing were introduced into their technology and conduct. Some of the excitement surrounding the great ceremonies evaporated and they lost their previous gaiety and interest" (*Human Organization*, pp. 17-22). Missionaries, who thought they were helping the aboriginals, unwittingly did much to dissolve the cultural glue that had sustained the group since time immemorial.

The problem the case illustrates is that actions, no matter how well meant, often have an impact far beyond intention. The lesson it suggests is that **any** action intended to bring about change must be framed within a holistic appreciation of the wider context.

To truly get to grips with the new role, the promoted or newly arriving executive must first "get behind the mask;" he/she must strip away the public face of the organization and find out what is really driving the business. Even where the executive is faced with the same but expanded role he/she is strongly advised to revisit this fundamental question. In truth, without a sound understanding of the forces propelling the business forward, the new executive is left with little more than history, rumor, story and advice from others as the platform upon which to build a personal agenda.

The challenge for the new executive is to find a meaningful passage through what can be perilous seas. Critical to that journey is defining the role and agreeing on priorities. The executive cannot, however, define the new role without first understanding the wider organizational implications and strategic imperatives. To do so is to assume, metaphorically, that stone axes no longer have worth.

This notion of understanding what drives the company has a forbidding tone to it, especially if the new executive is in, say, a branch plant or somewhere else remote from the organization's center. After all, how can someone new to the organization truly understand the strategic thinking that underlies the organization's long-term direction? How can someone who didn't sit in on the strategy sessions get a real feel for what was discussed?

Alternatively, the executive who has been promoted within an organization may feel he or she already understands what drives it – "After all, I've been here ten years!" Well, those ten years, while giving them the experience and expertise responsible for their promotion, may well have done much to blind them to the big picture and its processes. And, in the case of an executive undergoing merger or acquisition, it may be very true that what drove the business yesterday is in the backseat today.

The executive's understanding of the business drivers can be greatly helped if he or she can get a hold of the strategy documents and, where possible, talk to those who were responsible for their composition. It is also important to remember that coming fresh to strategic issues can be an advantage. A recently arrived executive, or an executive in a new role within his old organization, is seeing with new eyes; he or she is not locked into past thinking and past patterns of behavior. The executive in a new role also has the advantage of being able to tap his/her own past strategic work. This is especially valuable if the previous experience was with a competitor, or a successful division within the current enterprise.

Exploring and analyzing what drives the organization is an important issue in terms of fit and managing expectations. It is also a significant factor in determining how the executive in a new role starts to make a contribution.

Figure 11 – What Drives the Business - explores the landscape of strategy and implementation faced by the executive moving into a new role.

A natural and healthy consequence of stepping back to view the overall strategic panorama is that the new executive will (and should) start to form some of his or her own opinions. These early judgments will surface as part of both defining the role and in establishing a strategic agenda. The place to start, however, is not with how the new executive believes the world **should be** but with an **accurate assessment of how it is now**.

What follows focuses on the areas of the overall strategic picture that an executive moving into a new role cannot afford to push aside: stakeholders' and shareholders' expectations,

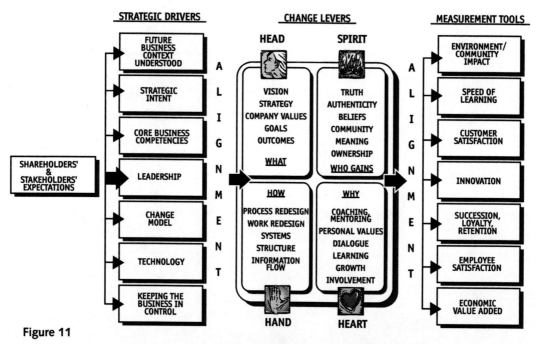

Figure 11

WHAT DRIVES THE BUSINESS?

the business drivers, the change enablers and the tools the organization accesses to measure success.

Shareholders' and stakeholders' expectations

The market place is invariably the final arbiter of success for the modern organization. Shareholders vote with their feet or, more accurately, their investment portfolio. Even privately held or family businesses cannot ignore the forces at play in the capital markets.

The incoming or promoted executive, regardless of level or role, needs to become very familiar with the market's perception of the organization. He or she should become aware of the history of share price fluctuations, analysts' reports, and press releases from and coverage about the company.

Today's ease of access to sources like databases, friendly brokerages, the Internet, and the financial press all make seeing the organization through the eyes of a shareholder relatively straightforward.

Understanding stakeholder expectations is clearly more complex. The first order of business is simply to determine who the key stakeholders are. Unions, suppliers, customers and employees are all unquestionably important stakeholders. Other key stakeholders are subtler in their relationship to an organization. For instance, a mining company's stakeholders might include indigenous native groups, or, a business that works with potentially hazardous material might need to see the local populous as a concerned party.

Walking the boundaries of the organization, as discussed in Chapter one, establishes a feel for the needs of suppliers and customers.

But coming to an understanding of, say, the union's longer term concerns is a little more difficult because issues of principle and philosophy won't register in the nuts and bolts of contracts or collective agreements. This raises the question: is it important for the promoted or incoming executive to know what the union's concerns are if he or she does not have direct contact with it? Let me try to answer that question with an anecdote. A marketing executive I know, during his first week in a new position, spoke at a conference. In his speech, he made the sort of remarks he had always made. However, when the remarks filtered back to the union through press coverage, they inflamed a sensitive union issue about which he had been totally unaware.

Regardless of position or role, it is always smart to find out how other key stakeholders feel about things. In a union environment, part of any constituency building should include discussions with the industrial-relations team.

There is a wealth of information available about employees if the new executive knows where to look for it. Climate surveys, focus groups, town hall meetings, and exit interviews, all provide invaluable background information. With or without these, however, the new executive must find the time to talk to people across the organization to get a sense of spirit, morale, and energy.

What drives this business?

Short-term thinking, combined with a psychological need for executives to feel they are "making things happen," means that few organizations spend the time to truly understand the organization's strategic drivers. Even a cursory study of the work of top teams reveals that short-term problems tend to dominate such that there is little time left for true strategic dialogue. It is too easily displaced to the obligatory and less productive annual strategic retreat. And, even then, an external facilitator typically sets the agenda, so the quality of debate is often constrained by the "packaged" strategic planning process.

Strategic thinking should be the **primary** role of the top team. The result of neglecting such long-term strategy is a misplaced confidence in the "quick fix." Process reengineering, teamwork, information systems, the process organization, TQM, building scorecards, and a host of other processes have all been expertly "sold" with little apparent concern about the fit with the organization's strategic realities e.g. culture.

Alignment is a much-heralded term – but you have to align **with** something. Without an understanding of the organization's strategic drivers, what is referred to as alignment is, at best, vague. The executive in a new role cannot afford this ambiguity when it comes to building a platform for success.

Seven business drivers, in particular, are pivotal: understanding the future business context, strategic intent, the organization's core business competencies, leadership, the need for a change model, the key technologies, and keeping the business under control.

The future business context

When the top executives of this generation are evaluated, what will separate the great from the merely good will not be things like financial engineering or marketing skills. The true measure of executive success is likely to be a much rarer attribute: the ability to anticipate how tomorrow will unfold.

The executive in a new role needs to start to explore the patterns of strategic change that are likely to shape tomorrow's business success from day one.

Three critical questions frame this understanding: (1) What breakthrough social, economic and/or political forces are likely to change the way the organization does business? (2) What market/customer/technology shifts are likely to irrevocably change the competitive landscape? And, (3) what internal forces are emerging that will change dramatically the way those in key leadership roles will need to think about the business?

None of the above questions exists in isolation – impact one and all three are affected. Like a stone hitting the windscreen of a moving car, although the initial crack may appear only at the point of initial impact it takes but moments before the whole has been transformed.

As the new executive wrestles with the complexity and challenge of his/her new role these three questions should be constantly running in the background. There may be no ready and easy answers. The value lies less in the answers, however, than it does in that by returning to these questions the new executive is constantly filtering and validating the information he/she is given against a broader sense of the social earthquakes, market fissures, and business dilemmas that the organization is likely to have to respond to as it steps forward.

Strategic intent

Strategic intent is simply a means to describe how the organization anticipates it will provide value for tomorrow's customer.

Every business needs to be able to answer one simple customer question: why should we use you? In a competitive world the answer should be second nature, and the person asked should be able to present, in unambiguous terms, how his or her organization differentiates itself from the competition. It is a question that, surprisingly enough, few organizations can answer with clarity.

Differentiation implies that one organization offers intrinsic value not offered by another. Describing that value can accurately be called the winning value proposition. Adding to that value is value advancement. Value advancement implies three things: (1) the supplier can deliver the increased value promised; (2) the value can be delivered consistently and in an uninterrupted manner; (3) and the promised additional value is something that the customer or client would be willing to pay for.

A winning value proposition describes **what** is offered – the head; identifies **how** the value will be delivered – the hand; captures the **passion and commitment** that support the offering – the heart; and gives a clear understanding of **who gains** – the spirit.

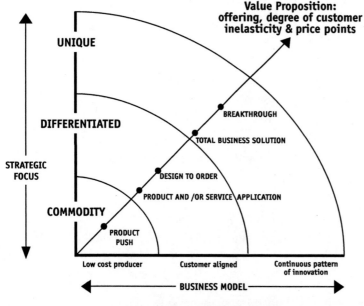

Figure 12

THE VALUE LADDER

Value is invariably created as an output of three core processes: (1) the offering process (the price and utility of the product or service); (2) the serving process (the customer's emotional experience buying and living with the product or service); (3) the distribution process (the customer's access to the product or service). There is only one meaningful way to measure or evaluate value: from **the customer's perspective**.

An example of strategic intent defined as value creation is outlined in **Figure 12**. It describes incremental value steps, the strategic focus demanded and the supporting business model.

Understanding the organization's strategic intent is of help to the promoted or incoming executive as a preface to defining the role he or she is to assume. It also starts to provide an anchor point for aligning the levers of change. For example, the organization structure, information technology and the compensation system must all reflect and reinforce the organization's emerging value proposition.

Core business competencies

Core competencies describe what it is that the organization does **uniquely** well. A core competency represents ideas, processes, people, technologies and shared learning that, when bundled together, provide the basis for **sustainable** competitiveness. More often than not, the organization's core competency lies not in any or even all of the parts, but in **how** they are brought together. A world-class chef needs first class ingredients but greatness lies not simply in the quality of the produce but in the way the elements are combined.

In their landmark *Harvard Business Review* article (May-June 1990), Prahalad and Hamel describe three characteristics of an organization's core business competency. The first: the core competency provides potential access to a wide variety of markets. The second: the core competency should make a significant contribution to the customer's perception of the benefits of the end product. The third: a core competency should be difficult for a competitor to imitate.

Examples of core competencies become quickly apparent when one examines organizations that have been historically best in class. For example, Toyota's process, manufacturing and engineering skills, Perkins Engine's capability in application engineering, Caterpillar's ability to deliver 24-hour service, Disney's creative animation, Sony's capacity to miniaturize, 3M's product development, Corning's skills in specialty glass, and the ability of those within Federal Express to make information technology serve the customer, are all core competencies that others have found tough to compete with.

Identifying core business competencies helps answer a number of key questions. Do we have the capability to deliver the intended value proposition? What should we keep and what should we outsource? When things get tough, what should we protect? What new markets should the organization target? What experience is essential for high-potential employees? What should the corporate center nurture? Where does the real power lie?

The incoming or promoted executive should explore the following ten questions when thinking about the organization's core competencies:

1. What process or activity within the organization would be virtually impossible to outsource?

2. What is it about us that our competition fears most?   Where is the magic?

3. What part of the organization has the highest number of high-potential employees? When a key employee leaves where is there the greatest degree of concern?

4. What part of the organization's capability would be most difficult for the competition to replicate?

5. Which employees in the organization would be the most difficult to replace?

6. Whose presentation is most eagerly anticipated at the annual conference?

7. Where, in the organization, are the mavericks tolerated (and why)?

8. What part of the organization have those on the top team been drawn from?

9. When the company beats out a world-class competitor for a key sale, what were the "buy" criteria?

10. If you could personally own one piece of the organization, which slice would it be?

Leadership

Like much in the last twenty-five years, leadership is a feature of business life that has seen a great deal of change. These changes have been written about, philosophized, in some instances eulogized and at other times seen as yet one more fad.

For the executive moving into a new role, understanding the leadership challenge goes without saying. That there are many ways to describe leadership is a redundant statement. Of those numerous paths, exploring leadership from the perspective of value creation draws out a pragmatic understanding that more philosophical descriptions lack.

Until the late 1970s, leadership from an Anglo Saxon perspective was pretty consistent: make the systems complex and the jobs simple; break jobs down into their smallest constituent part, and let the accountants rule. It was a world of kiss up and kick down. *It was leadership primarily of things.*

In the 1980s, the need for global competitiveness, combined with the Deming-inspired North American quality revolution, led to a rethinking of the basic premise upon which the modern organization was founded: the need for hierarchy. The name of the game became, as one writer put it, "toppling the Pyramid." It was also the era when organizations realized that the quality of the product or service was not enhanced through the expediency of more control, but by better understanding the nature and efficiency of the organization's core **business processes**. Complex systems and simple jobs were replaced by the need to simplify the systems and enrich the jobs. Enter stage left: empowerment, mass customization, service excellence, process reengineering, and a host of other tools and techniques. *Leadership dominated by a perceived need to manage boundaries was replaced with leadership approach that focused on behavior. The white space on the organization chart became more important than the boxes.*

The 60s and 70s had been an era where dominance lay with the producer: if we make it they will come. It was a business world where transaction ruled: the dominant competitive force was price. The 80s saw product quality and the nature of the service becoming a factor and, with it, a move from transaction as the basis of customer value to a focus on fit with customer needs. It was a period when listening to the customer came of age. Focus on *process improvement*, and a heightened level of agility was the response to this "new" understanding.

In the 1990s, the game changed yet again. Globalization, excess production capacity as a result of productivity gains, information technology and its twin handmaidens variety and choice, all combined to make the customer/consumer king. The new challenge: customer value. Leading edge firms started to realize that the knowledge and expertise that lay with the customer and/or supplier were potentially part of the overall "offering."

Moreover, in an age where focus on "the process" was proving to be a valuable strategy, there were unexploited opportunities for the supplier beyond the traditional product or service offering. By focusing on *process innovation* and a fuller understanding of the end-to-end value chain, by breaking down the barriers between supplier, producer and customer, and by seeking new ways to bring value to the customer (service contracts, shared funding on R & D projects, outsourcing, consulting support, learning collaboratives, shared databases and systems etc.), a product/service focus gives way to "a total (business) solution." *The leadership imperative: competitive differentiation through knowledge creation. The white space now expands to embrace a whole lot of other people's white space.*

Where are we headed? The next generation of value creation moves beyond "response" and starts to access concepts, connections and intellectual capital as the means to compete. Leveraging idea creation, innovation and knowledge, businesses will "invent" ways to create value for the customer's customer that the customer is unaware of. The emerging leadership imperative: an ability to continuously reinvent the game. The color and form of the "space" is limited only by the imagination of those involved.

The new executive can only define the leadership model he/she will be expected to execute if there is an understanding of the "value mind-set." This alone is not enough, however; successful organizations must constantly revisit their means to create value. What works today will be inappropriate tomorrow. The new executive needs to understand not merely today's leadership need but the self-development challenge that lies ahead.

Change model

A change model is a simple map of the change journey. It introduces common language. A well thought through change model becomes the container within which meaningful dialogue echoes. It provides imagery that engages. It links the thinking organization with the doing organization and it transforms that which would otherwise be complex into something that front-line employees want to run with. Few organizations build their change initiatives around a common change model. Then again, at least 90% of organizations attempting to orchestrate large-scale change fail!

A number of change models have come (in some instances, back) into focus during the past decade. Socio-tech thinking, a quality approach based on Deming's fourteen principles, six sigma, workout, balanced scorecard, Elliott Jaques' Requisite Organization, and Daryl

Conner's burning platform all outline different ways to look at change. The author's T1, T2, T3 model would be yet one more change model.

Ideally, an organization should build its own map of change. Regardless of the authorship, those responsible should bear in mind that **one** change model is better than **several** that compete.

The thinking behind the change model should reflect and be aligned with the other key strategic drivers. Equally important, **before** you go out and hire a "top gun" consultant to help you orchestrate change, find out what tools he or she carries in their holster. Think twice before hiring someone who is not in tune with the philosophy already in place elsewhere in the organization. And no matter what conceptual package for change you settle on, insist that **leadership** of the change process stays with you and in no way passes to the consultant.

Value creation is more than a passing fad. And value advancement is not merely a matter of pushing ahead and hoping for the best. Those who seek to move beyond a product solution formula will find that the traditional hierarchical structure limits what is possible. Similarly, those wanting to move even further into true innovation and opportunity creation will discover that the most limiting barrier is likely to be the lack of a supportive culture.

If there is a poor understanding of what is involved in change, and/or there is little or no real dialogue around culture, the organization will falter and those involved will be incapable of really understanding why.

Regardless of the change model(s) in vogue within the organization, the executive in a new role needs to find out as much as he or she can about the approach in question. Ignorance of, for example, Elliott Jaque's ideas and methodology will not only exclude the executive from much of the discussion around levels of decision-making but could, as a result, handicap the executive's ability to meaningfully define his or her role.

Leadership is about change. Meaningful change doesn't happen by chance. Somewhere in the change agenda there has to be a conceptual plan, a unique teaching point of view, a way to bring meaning to the otherwise chaotic patterns and shapes that make for leadership of change. The change schema may not amount to more than a few phrases or a simple metaphor. Alternatively, it might well follow one of the "models" previously identified e.g. six sigma. Identifying the change model(s) being used is for the leader akin to someone taking possession of a new car; it will only operate – no matter how skilled the driver – if he/she first has access to the key that opens the driver's door.

Technology

The organization's core business competencies describe what it is the organization does uniquely well. In many instances, an organization's technology is integral to its core competency.

For instance, supporting, developing and marketing Microsoft's operating system has clearly been its historical core competency. IMAX, the film format, lies at the center of the creative approach to business development taken by the Toronto-based organization that developed the process.

Understanding the organization's technology is important to the promoted or incoming executive even if it is not at the center of the organization's core business competency e.g. a consulting company. Much of the company's history can only be understood by following the evolution of its technology. By building insight into *evolving* technologies, the new executive is better able to think about new markets and next generation customers. Moreover, knowing how new products are developed and how innovation is nurtured allows the new executive to follow to its source the creative spark that represents the basis of potential future wealth creation.

Water finds its way to the sea by finding and following the easiest route. For similar reasons the executive in a new role cannot afford to overlook the role of Information Technology in the new role. IT introduces new, easy and convenient ways for people within the organization to communicate. Information technology creates what quickly become the established communication channels. The tricky stuff comes when these new channels are at odds with the formal means to communicate as established by the formal organization structure. The resulting tension can be a major source of internal conflict if it is not understood and responded to effectively.

There have been essentially three waves of technology. Wave one brought the word processor and a range of technology-based tools aimed at improving individual *efficiency*. Wave two gave us connectivity, group ware, Multi-media, and the Internet - information technology based on *creating and sharing* knowledge. The third wave of technology makes use of seamless intelligence gathering, smart systems, and artificial intelligence to *create new ways to be*.

The first wave, from a cultural perspective, is an appropriate fit within a traditional, hierarchical organization i.e., improving the efficiency and productivity of the pyramid. The second wave of technology enhances performance in those organizations where process thinking dominates. Information technology, as a new way to be, appropriately drives those organizations where continuous innovation, real-time response and perpetual opportunity creation, move to the fore.

Technologies in general and information technology in particular, are essential pieces of the integration puzzle. The new executive who fails to recognize this and who does not take time out to understand the role of technology and its impact on his/her new role is putting his/her long-term success at risk.

Keeping the business under control

When you try to take a sharp corner in a car, you wouldn't think about taking your hands off the wheel. Organizations need the same kind of control to negotiate the curves. The executive moving into a new role needs to know what and how his or her car is kept on the road; he or she must understand the organization's tools for control.

Many of these tools are financial in focus. For instance, budget control, EBIT, RONA, ROCE, inventory turns, cash flow, sales, market share, and working capital are all methods used to steer an organization. A high percentage of organizations complement financial measures with a focus on key ratios: employees to sales, information technology cost as a percentage of sales, number of grievances in the pipeline, recruitment lag, turnover, employee attitude, learning, speed to market, measures of innovation, intellectual capital, and customer satisfaction. Others yet again have moved to measure the level of Economic Value Added and, through it, monitor not only business performance but also the quality of leadership being brought to bear.

The simple reality is that organizations, of necessity, *focus on what it is they measure*. The inevitable consequence of this is that the organization's key measurement tools play a major role in driving the business forward. The measurement tools also become the fundamental means to evaluate success - after the event. This relationship between strategy and measurement is best understood by viewing figure eleven as being cyclic. The result: measuring the *right outcomes* allows those in key roles to better understand and thus adjust/change the organization's strategic drivers.

As with technology, understanding these measures is absolutely essential for an executive moving into a new role. *It is an imperative no matter what function or specialization the new executive is in*. If you are not familiar with the means and techniques to measure performance used by the organization, addressing this shortfall must become a critical priority. The challenge is not to become a financial expert overnight. Having said that, in order not to spin out, the promoted or incoming executive **must** become familiar with both the ongoing controls and the way that they are calculated.

The need for balance

There are many models of leadership and indeed many passionate advocates to make a case for each. If there is one thread that runs through most, if not all, of the more pragmatic examples it is that sustainable, authentic, and successful leadership is ultimately about *balance*.

An executive moving into a new role must understand the organization's strategic drivers. Exploring how the organization creates customer value is central to knowing *how the business does business*. Core business competencies provide an invaluable frame of reference about future market opportunity. And knowing how the business measures success is an important part of establishing the characteristics of *personal* success.

Then we come to the topic of change. Change in the way it is enacted by the vast majority of organizations builds on interventions that are anchored in the *head* and the *hand*. Stretch targets, new strategies and a focus on the organization's values become the clarion call. The means to achieve these goals, it is invariably suggested, is through a focus on reengineering processes, new technology, cost cutting, reorganization, and better training. These all represent important leadership work but they do not meet the essential test of *balance*.

The *head* and the *hand* address the *what* and the *how*. What is missing is the *why* (heart) and *who gains* (spirit)? An executive moving into a new role cannot afford to ignore the issue of *balance*. He/she cannot hope to succeed if he/she ignores the need to engage the *heart* and enrich the *spirit* of those he/she inherits and works along side.

Leadership of the heart must come from the heart. It is a form of leadership that builds dialogue as a natural part of how people work together. It is an approach to change that recognizes the role of the leader as mentor and coach. It is a pattern of behavior that focuses on the importance of people's personal values and the role of learning as a means to compete. It is a way to be that shapes the tension in the organization such that the team comes to accept that being at the edge is essential if best in class aspirations are to be realized. An executive moving into a new role cannot afford to ignore the importance of *balance*.

Spirit speaks of engagement at an even deeper level. The executive who understands how to touch the spirit of the team will never walk alone. Spirit demands truth. Spirit is drawn out of authenticity. Spirit is built on openness and the power of community. Spirit draws on the meaning and worth in the work being undertaken. Spirit connects. Spirit is anchored in courage: the courage to say I was wrong; to admit I don't know; to give honest feedback; to be honest with one's self. Spirit is displayed in the courage to admit to mistakes and move on. The inevitable conclusion: without spirit there is no *balance*!

* * * * *

A mountain runner who had enjoyed a number of victories was once asked the key to competitive success. He replied, "keep your eye on the mountain, not on the runner in front of you."

The new executive is faced with a learning agenda that can be overwhelming. "Runners," in many guises, will vie to gain his or her attention. Ignoring those needs is not always possible. But the promoted or incoming executive must above all, keep his or her eye on the mountain - *understand what drives the business and strive for balance.*

Chapter Four

Critical Learning

- The new executive must understand the wider organizational and strategic imperatives.

- Before exploring what drives the business, the new executive must understand the shareholders' and stakeholders' expectations.

- The key to defining what drives the business lies in the following: the future business context; the organization's strategic intent; the core business competencies; leadership; the change model around which the organization articulates and defines the change journey; technology; and how the business is kept under control.

- Leadership is about balancing the head, the hand, the heart, and the spirit.

Consequences

Even though they may have been outlined as part of the recruitment process, the new executive must be absolutely certain that he/she understands specifically what the business is all about. Without this "due diligence" the new executive is, metaphorically, heading into heavy seas without a map and a compass. Without an understanding of what drives the business, the new executive is poorly positioned to define the role.

Step back and reflect on the ideas that surfaced and the learning you take from this chapter. Consider the path you are on, the need to build relationships (fit), and your understanding of success in the new role (expectations). Think about what you need to stop doing, start doing, and that which you need to do differently.

Defining the new role

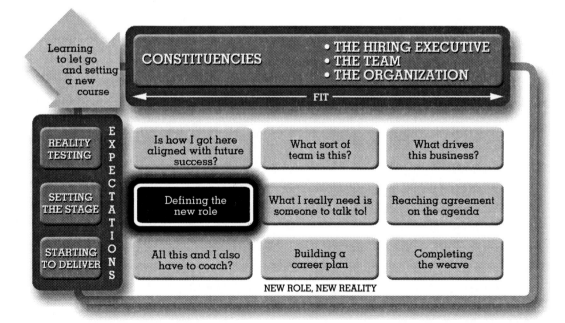

Learning to let go and setting a new course

CONSTITUENCIES	• THE HIRING EXECUTIVE
	• THE TEAM
	• THE ORGANIZATION

←———————————————— FIT ————————————————→

	E	Is how I got here aligned with future success?	What sort of team is this?	What drives this business?
REALITY TESTING	X P E C T A T I O N S			
SETTING THE STAGE		**Defining the new role**	What I really need is someone to talk to!	Reaching agreement on the agenda
STARTING TO DELIVER		All this and I also have to coach?	Building a career plan	Completing the weave

NEW ROLE, NEW REALITY

Defining the new role

In the "good old days," you were handed a job description, instructed as to how to behave and told "stay in your box." And it worked - in a steady-state world built on assumptions of predictability. Well that was then and this is now. Welcome to the new century, where anxious ambiguity about your role is the prevailing condition. That does not mean that ambiguity is the same as freestyle chaos. You still need to build a meaningful definition of the role you are about to assume or as one writer elegantly put it, "a river without banks is a swamp."

Early settlers in Australia thought the aboriginals were nomadic because they lacked a concept of land ownership. Bruce Chatwell, in *The Songlines*, argues that "this was nonsense. Aboriginals, it was true, could not imagine territory as a block of land hemmed in by frontiers, but rather as an interlocking network of lines or ways through."

The genesis of aboriginal thinking about territory lay in the reality that the Australian outback was essentially a huge scrub-filled desert where life-sustaining levels of rainfall fell only about once every seven years. To stay in one place was thus suicidal. Chatwell goes on to explain that, to an aboriginal, a man's "own country" was not defined by location, but was "the place where I do not have to ask." This perception of space, a kind of cultural memory, was built from ten thousand generations of adaptive mastery.

Like it or not, the rest of us don't have quite that amount of time available. And yet we are being called upon to adapt. The ponderous, hierarchical geographically-bounded organizations created a hundred or more years ago have little, if any, relevance to the needs of an enterprise that to survive must operate globally, respond to opportunity at the speed of light, and leverage knowledge as the basis of competitiveness. Put simply, success in the organizations of the Twenty-First Century demands that each of us reframe our definition of "territory." To endure, let alone thrive, we must develop a sense of space dominated not by "the fence" but by a belief that the way forward lies in continuously expanding one's area of awareness, influence, and contribution. The world we are entering is far more about Songlines than it is about straight lines. Organizational agility ultimately defines a place where "I do not have to ask."

For three generations the ubiquitous job description has been the accepted way to stake out the boundaries defining work activity. A command and control philosophy suggests that efficiency is maximized when workers are given small, easy to learn pieces of the productive process. The idea behind such carefully defined work boundaries is to minimize job overlap. Implicit in this belief that man works best when being told what to do is the supposition that innovation, "ownership," and response to change are best left to a select few of the deserving and trusted.

There is of course another point of view: that in order to compete in a business world dominated by uncertainty and rapidly unfolding opportunity, an organization must unlock **all** of its resources, particularly the intellect, enthusiasm and commitment of those who deal on a day-to-day basis with the customer.

Simple and obvious as a "close to the customer" scenario may seem, it is only possible if those in key leadership roles are prepared to give up the comfort of rules, policies, manuals, procedures – all those wonderful "directives" that make it oh so easy to place blame (elsewhere) when things go wrong.

The job description has served its purpose. It was a tool for its time. The challenge: in a world where change is the norm, what takes its place? Does self-organization mean that decision-making has been displaced to those who have, regardless of background and competency, the courage to act? Or, is there a need to make consensus a mandatory component of virtually every decision?

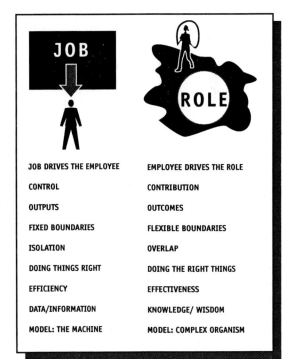

JOB	ROLE
JOB DRIVES THE EMPLOYEE	EMPLOYEE DRIVES THE ROLE
CONTROL	CONTRIBUTION
OUTPUTS	OUTCOMES
FIXED BOUNDARIES	FLEXIBLE BOUNDARIES
ISOLATION	OVERLAP
DOING THINGS RIGHT	DOING THE RIGHT THINGS
EFFICIENCY	EFFECTIVENESS
DATA/INFORMATION	KNOWLEDGE/ WISDOM
MODEL: THE MACHINE	MODEL: COMPLEX ORGANISM

Figure 13

What is certain is that, for the executive tackling a new role, nothing is more stressful and disruptive than not knowing what is expected.

William Bridges' vision of the world beyond the job description provides part of the answer. In *Job Shift*, Bridges looks toward a world without jobs: a world where more and more people will work in organizations where the work arrangements are "too fluid and idiosyncratic to be called jobs."

The need for fluidity is added to by Mihaly Csikszentmihalyi's recognition of the boredom factor: if there is not change and workable challenge he said, "we grow either bored or frustrated; and then the desire to enjoy ourselves again pushes us to stretch our skills, or to discover new opportunities for using them."

Arguably, the rest of the answer lies within our own sense of challenge and the organizational context we find ourselves in. On one hand, we have to recognize that the world of the tightly defined job is redundant and largely dysfunctional. On the other, unless the promoted or incoming executive can develop some insight, some sense of shared meaning, about his or her *role* (above and beyond *'the job'*), confusion and a cry for help cannot be far behind. **See Figure 13**.

The pragmatic reality: for the new executive, meaningfully defining his or her role becomes an absolute imperative if he or she is to thrive in fluid and dynamic organization forms, and if he or she is to build a meaningful platform for personal success. If there is one overriding lesson drawn from those who stumble during the integration period it is that there is nothing more important than building agreement over the shape, scope and nature of the new role.

But defining the role is not like painting a house: do it and forget about it for five years. The role must be seen as a platform for evolving success where continued success requires continuous adaptation to an ever-changing environment.

Life was comfortable when we were handed a job description and, in essence, told what we could and couldn't do. Play by the rules, make the boss look good, and failure was relatively easy to avoid. Avoiding failure, however, is not the same as being successful. By shaping the nature of our work, and by pushing to the edge of our own comfort zone, we not only open the door for heightened contribution, but we increase the likelihood of failure.

This is never truer than when we either move into a new role or when the role we have changes significantly. The following thoughts and insights about role definition have been drawn out of in-depth discussion with those undergoing role transition.

Remember, the map is never the territory; the suggestions here are necessarily incomplete. They do, however, outline and capture what a wide range of executives moving into new roles have learned through and about this frequently confusing and frustrating period of transition.

Defining the new role starts with an understanding of leadership.

Most modern organizations seem to believe that those in power hold the reins because they know what it takes to be a leader. The world makes sense this way. Because of this faith, leadership as a philosophy is rarely an agenda item even among top management teams.

But, for the executive moving into a new role, determining what successful leadership in the "new" organization looks like is a key factor in answering that all too important question: what is my role?

Knowing where to look for leadership is not as easy as it once was. It's no longer simply a matter of taking a stroll down mahogany row and measuring egos. In a world where decision-making has been pushed closer to the customer, where organizations have of necessity become more responsive, where the traditional leadership pyramid has been flattened, leadership must thrive at every level of the organization.

Leadership begins with a purpose: Why are we here? What is our mission? What wouldn't get done if we did not exist?

Direction is rooted in the mission. But a mission is only compelling, able to move people, if it is complemented by a vibrant, lucid, full-bodied, and richly worded, vision.

"Vision" in this sense is a very distant cousin to the "vision statement" (an oxymoron if ever there was one). A vision that moves people appeals to the heart. A vision transforms. A vision takes what can be and turns it into a reality. A vision paints tomorrow so vividly that those who are drawn to it, those who share it, are driven by it. A vision makes the future come alive. A vision takes people places that otherwise they would not go. Conversely, the absence of a vision is tacit permission to do what has always been done.

A compelling vision anchors a winning strategy. If you're given no reason to go, and no sense that you'll find what you want when you get there, then you'll resist even a simple journey. And if they're expecting you to cross interstates and take sandy back roads, then, with their reasons and incentives, they sure as hell better provide a route map. In business, as in war, the "map" is manifest as the strategy.

An effective strategy is built on three domains of effectiveness: the **CUSTOMER**, the **COMPANY**, and the **COMPETITION**. **See Figure 14**. To be strategic means that the following questions have been answered: (1) who are tomorrow's customers and what are their emerging needs? (**CUSTOMER**); (2) what is it that we do uniquely well as a company to create value, and is that capability aligned with the needs of tomorrow's customers? (**COMPANY**); (3) what is the most damaging thing our (potential) competitors could do and how do we do it first? (**COMPETITION**). Strategy that fails to answer these three fundamental questions can be described as a highly expensive form of wishful thinking. Organizations spend a lot of money on wishful thinking.

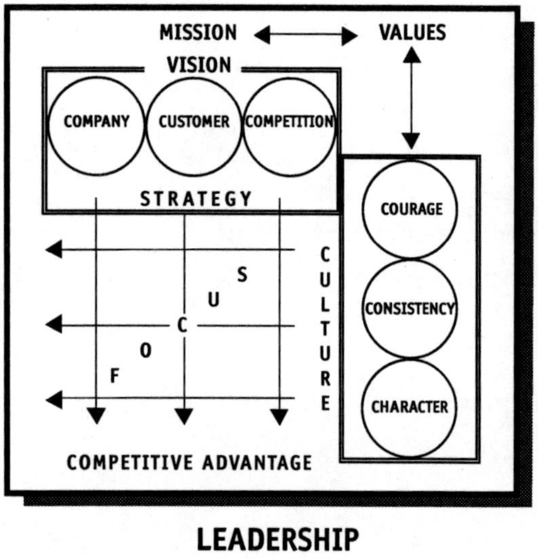

Many businesses, of course, develop a well thought through strategy but still fail. This leads us to the next critical building block of leadership: values.

Leaders, real leaders, lead not through conjecture, suggestion, hyperbole, threat, or the naked use of power, but through example. They behave the way they want

LEADERSHIP

Figure 14

others to behave. When Sam Walton traveled coach and stayed at low-budget hotels he wasn't displaying a mean streak; he was defining what it was that Wal-Mart had to do to deliver its value proposition of always being the low cost producer. Andrew Grove, the man who made Intel a technological powerhouse, works from a 2.5.m by 2.7m cubicle.

In *Corporate Pathfinders*, Harold J. Leavitt frames values most succinctly: "People in authority are always under the spotlight in an organization. Their actions, often distorted and caricatured, are quickly telegraphed and carefully dissected in a search for hidden meanings and purposes that often aren't there. Over time those interpretations are distilled into a picture of the "real" values of this company, to be adopted or attacked depending on the larger organizational culture" (90).

The executive moving into a new role needs to understand that all those in leadership roles live under the microscope. The higher you are in the enterprise, the larger the lens through which you are viewed. The message: employees learn what successful behavior is not by listening to what leaders say, but **from watching what leaders do.**

Is this a new concept? Well, Moctezuma Xocoyotzin, the last great Aztec ruler, was said to personify "the ideals, beliefs of his culture in his exemplary behavior as well as in his physical appearance" (*Aztec,* Jane S. Day, 1992). So some have figured it out.

Because strategy is constantly evolving, it is not, and cannot be, the glue that holds all the pieces in place. **Commitment**, ongoing **consistency**, and the source of **courage** when faced with adversity come from a shared purpose. They are amplified and made real through a belief in, and fervent adherence to, a set of values.

The Romans built an empire on a strategy of conquer and integrate. Behind their victories, however, lay the power of the Roman legion, the finest fighting force the world had ever seen. The lowest common denominator of the legions was the contubernium - eight man units (maximum occupancy of a campaign tent) that lived, ate and slept together. The Romans rarely moved men between units because they realized that when all was said and done the men did not fight for the glory of the empire - they fought for each other! Leadership is, at heart, about the change journey. It is an emotional pilgrimage to tomorrow that seeks to frame why those taking the journey are doing so, what the new world has to offer, and the best route to get there. However, when everything else is stripped away, people don't follow the strategy, they follow a leader. They don't fight for the glory of the organization - they fight for each other.

Leaders move people to the edge

A hundred years ago rural life depended on the skills of the village blacksmith. He fixed farm implements, shod horses, repaired carriages, and made a range of articles needed for rural existence, including nails, door hinges, and knives. His work involved tremendous strength, an extraordinary level of hand/eye coordination, and, of course, judgment.

The role also allowed for a certain level of artistic flair. Metal taken from the forge, often immersed in water or oil, was moved to the anvil. At the anvil the cherry red metal was beaten and shaped into form. To anyone watching, his skills and judgment were easy to overlook. For those who understood the trade, it was apparent that if the metal was left too long in the forge, it could not be worked. Those so informed also understood that the smith was striking the anvil with a tactile dexterity born out of years of practice. The secret to knowing when the metal was at the right heat lay in the smith's keen eye and sense of timing. His ear was attuned to the tone and pitch of metal striking metal. The wrong temperature or the wrong pressure, and instead of producing a finely wrought instrument, he had more scrap metal.

The smith's world reveals a great deal about leadership in today's context. We all learn most effectively at the edge of our comfort zone. The leader's challenge is to create the context within which each member of his/her team is learning but not overwhelmed, stretched but not broken, taken to cherry red heat but not beyond.

Leaders build self-esteem

Traditional approaches to management are based on the presumption that management intervenes rather than participates: "let me know if (when) things go wrong." This approach means that meaningful dialogue only takes place when an employee is on the defensive and when the "boss" is unlikely to have cause to lavish praise.

This philosophy thrives for several reasons: (1) it gives the boss a position of interpersonal dominance; (2) it provides an opportunity for blame to be (dis)placed squarely "where it belongs;" and, (3) it places, from the employee's viewpoint, a perverse value on being able to keep the boss at arm's length.

During the annual performance discussion, this approach is dominated by the "gotcha" mentality. The result is a demoralizing experience where the majority of employees **have** to be informed that they are average, competent, or even worse, a 3.9 on a scale of 5.0.

By contrast, if value creation and "close to the customer" decision-making are the goals, those charged with making a difference have to have high feelings of self-worth.

Learning, risk, and personal growth are central to the development of self-esteem. Those who stay firmly entrenched in a world in which they feel safe have few resources to deal with new challenges. Such insecure people will withdraw, criticize, and use bargaining and grievance procedures to muddy the water.

The rate that an organization can expect to implement change is a factor of a number of variables (**see Figure 15**). Because of upbringing, culture, experience and temperament, not everyone has the same capacity to change (**C**). Someone going through divorce or the sickness of a child has little emotional energy left to deal with crisis at work. Such unresolved change (**U**) will distract and paralyze. Making available well-designed and holistic wellness programs is not just a way to general goodwill, but they can make for interventions that pay for themselves many times over.

Leaders do have an opportunity to influence the speed at which change unfolds. To take advantage of that opportunity, however, leadership has to move from "management **by** exception" to "management **of** exception." Because people don't resist change so much as being changed, leaders must give employees ownership of the processes (**D**) through which change is enacted, and they must aggressively look for ways to impact employee self-esteem (**S.E.**).

RATE OF CHANGE

$$RATE = S.E.(C - U) \times D$$

S.E. = self esteem
C = capacity for change
U = unresolved change
D = degree of ownership

Figure 15

Defining the new role is an absolutely essential dimension to hitting the ground running in a new role. And central to defining the role is seeing it from a **leadership perspective**. For this to be meaningful, leadership has to move from being an esoteric, academic concept to being something that the executive in a new role can explore pragmatically in terms of what it really means to him or her.

Defining the role must encompass the head, the hand, the heart and the spirit

There are four ways that any of us deal with the things that affect us: four dimensions of truth that lead to our understanding – the head, the hand, the heart and the spirit.

The first is derived from our ability to analyze an event or situation and to use our reasoning powers to *know* what is happening to us. *This is truth through knowing.*

The second involves our ability to reach out and physically investigate what touches our ongoing experience. *This is truth through doing.*

The third truth is drawn out of our emotions regarding the event or situation. *This is the truth through feeling.*

To find the fourth dimension of truth we must move beyond feelings to touch the very essence of who we are. *This is truth through being.* True wisdom lies at this fourth, and deepest, level of truth.

Key decisions such as, say, an acquisition that could change the fortunes of the organization, invariably involve all four truths. In the case of buying a business, the first step is to look through the books and assess the financial health of the target organization. The second action involves physically looking at the resources and talking to the people. So far so good: it looks right and it sounds right!   But does it feel right? Does it give the acquirer an inner sense that this is the right thing to do?

Anyone who has been involved with a seasoned professional during an acquisition quickly becomes aware that the ultimate decision rests as much with feelings and an intuitive sense of comfort than with the numbers. Merely knowing is not enough; true wisdom comes from tapping into **all four** levels of understanding (truth).

The executive in a new role should think about his role in a similar vein. Leadership that encompasses only the head and the hand presents a sterile and clinical profile that will do little to build loyalty and lasting commitment. Leadership that describes the systems and tools needed, but fails to describe why those being asked to follow should embark on the journey is a body without a heart. Leadership that does not enrich the human spirit is an attempt to build a house without mortar or a model airplane without glue – one won't hold and the other won't fly. If leadership is ultimately about mastery, leadership that relies on the head and hand isn't leadership at all but is, at best, an inadequate way to describe the act of managing. **See Figure 16.**

Defining the new role is something of a watershed for an executive during the integration period. Defining the role draws together all the executive has learned to this moment, including knowledge gained during the interview process, self-awareness regarding letting go, insights around culture, awareness concerning the stage of development of the new team, and understanding of the organization's strategic drivers. It is a watershed event because it also points the way forward.

Failing to think carefully about how the new role should unfold from a leadership perspective seriously handicaps the promoted or incoming executive.

What follows are the questions that a new executive should take into account when defining his or her new role. These should be considered as embryonic, a starting place or a first step. One needs to keep in mind that life is change and so one's role is ever evolving. Nonetheless, the questions outlined represent fundamental building blocks of understanding; not being able to answer one or more is a sign of potential misalignment that may well be the basis of conflict (often without the new executive being aware of it) with other members of the team.

Figure 16

Leadership context questions

- What key stakeholders does this role serve?

- What is the time horizon for the role? Is it largely strategic? Operational? Or tactical?

- How would a key customer describe the responsibilities encompassed by the role?

- How wide is the role's reach: countries, financial resources, support staff?

- What is the overall mission?

- Has the organization defined any overarching, company-wide leadership competencies?

- To what extent and how does this role influence/impact the speed at which the organization works? Is the current rhythm/cadence of action aligned with the customer's emerging needs?

- How would the immediate challenge in the role be described: Planter? Grower? Harvester? Turnaround?

The head (knowing) questions

- What is the vision for the role of the organization, the team, and the new executive? Are they aligned?

- How does this role impact on and deliver the organization's values?

- What key customers are served by this role?

- How would an ideal customer relationship be described?

- How is value created for the customer — today and tomorrow?

- What's the worst thing that could go wrong?

- If this job didn't exist, what wouldn't get done?

- What are the agreed performance expectations (outcomes) for the role: (1) quantitative (2) qualitative? See Chapter seven for more on agreeing the agenda.

- What key decisions are central to this role?

The hand (doing) questions

- What key customer processes does the role impact and how?

- What core internal processes does the role impact and how?

- What processes "owned" by suppliers does the role impact and how?

- To what extent, and how, does the role influence work redesign/product quality within the organization?

- To what extent, and how, does the role influence the way critical information flows along the value chain?

- How does the role impact the introduction/development of new products, services, and/or technology?

- How is the role influenced by the opportunities and potential that the Internet affords?

- How does the role shape the effectiveness of information technology?

- How does the role influence employee recruitment, retention, and commitment?

- What resources are needed to meet the outcomes (performance expectations) defined earlier?

The heart (feeling) questions

- To what extent does the new role have to span the following organizational forms: (1) traditional/hierarchical with the decisions made by few? **T1** (2) process driven where communication, decision-making, and teamwork are anchored in the organization's core business processes? **T2** (3) virtual, where processes, team assignments, and roles are constantly reconfigured to drive innovative responses to emerging market opportunity? **T3**

- With the three organizational points listed above in mind, what is the nature and scope of the challenge for this role in terms of managing change?

- With this role in mind, what future emphasis will be placed on coaching?

- Who is the focus of such coaching?

- How does the role contribute to the learning of others?

- With the scope of organizational change envisaged in mind, what and how is this role assumed to be central in gaining employee buy-in from employees?

The spirit (being) questions

- What is demanded of the role in terms of constituency building: Within the enterprise? Externally?

- What teams is the role involved with? What contribution is expected? What contribution is needed?

- Is the current team up to the challenge?

- What team leadership is demanded?

- How does the role contribute to a sense of community within the enterprise? Externally?

- How can the serving dimension of the role best be described? How is each of the key stakeholders served?

- How can the role positively contribute to the debate concerning such issues as affirmative action, diversity, sexual harassment, wellness, mentoring?

- How, while fulfilling this role, can I be a positive role model for others within the business, and within the community?

The questions outlined set the context for describing the new role. In practice the dialogue that supports better understanding of the role is, in many ways, as important as the role profile itself. Exploring the questions with the new team is an especially helpful dimension of defining the new role.

This is not to decry the value of separating the wheat from the chaff: establishing what elements of the role are absolutely vital and which are merely important.

A pragmatic outline of the role should

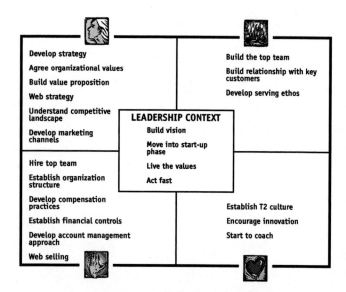

ROLE DEFINITION: PRESIDENT SMALL HIGH-TECH START UP

Figure 17

focus on relatively few critical areas of contribution. By establishing what is absolutely core to the role, the new executive is making a major step forward in terms of how he/she starts to focus time and resources.

A second contingency is to keep the areas of contribution simple – three to five words at most. Consider each area of contribution as a hands-on definition of where time and resources will make the greatest difference. At this stage the role definition should describe areas of accountability: the action points around which the role pivots. It goes without saying that a meaningful role definition balances head, hand, heart and spirit.

The behaviors aligned with success in the new role (competencies) should be carried out as a separate activity – see Chapter nine. **Figure 17** outlines the way the President of a small high-tech start-up went about defining his role. (A competency profile for this same role is outlined in Chapter nine.)

Many of the aboriginal tribes of North America believed that all animals, including man, had a dual existence. To them, a man could, at certain times, reveal his animal self. A bird or deer could, similarly, reveal that part of them that was man. Man and the animal kingdom took different forms but were in essence one.

Revealing one's other self was an intensely spiritual experience, and the means through which the warrior discovered his or her other form was the "vision quest."

"Vision quest" is also an appropriate term for the task of the incoming or promoted executive in the first weeks and months of a new role. In defining the role, he or she is also exploring the many parts that make up his or her true self.

To be effective and fulfilled, the new executive must move beyond a purely analytical and/or mechanistic view of the role and understand what it means to be a leader. He or she needs to be acutely aware of what it means to truly make a difference!

It is a journey of discovery that must capture both what leadership is and what leadership does. It is a quest that, if passion and commitment are to be more than just words, must engage not just the head and the hand, but the heart and the spirit.

Chapter Five

Critical Learning

- A role must be seen as a platform for excellence where continued success requires continuous adaptation to an ever-changing environment.
- Defining the role starts with a robust understanding of leadership.
- Leadership begins with the mission.
- A compelling vision anchors a winning strategy.
- Leadership and values are synonymous.
- Leaders move people to the edge.
- Leaders build self-esteem.
- A working definition of the new role must take account of the head, the hand, the heart, and the spirit.

Consequences

A role definition is a way to map out the scope and breadth of the leadership challenge on hand. An effective role definition must describe not only the "what" and the "how," but issues that explore the "why" and "who gains." A role definition that fails to encompass the heart and the spirit strips the new executive of much that is the very essence of leadership.

Step back and reflect on the ideas that surfaced and the learning you take from this chapter. Consider the path you are on, the need to build relationships (fit), and your understanding of success in the new role (expectations). Think about what you need to stop doing, start doing, and that which you need to do differently.

_____

_____

_____

_____

_____

_____

_____

_____

_____

_____

_____

What I really need is someone to talk to!

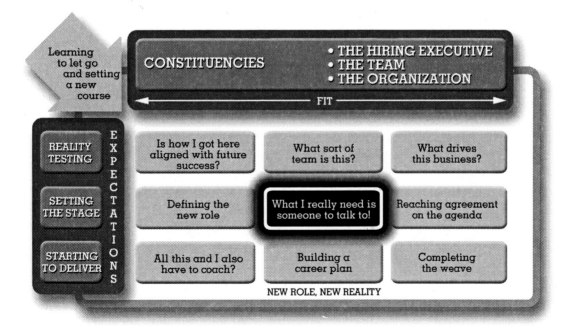

What I really need is someone to talk to

Walking into a new organization, or walking into a new role in a familiar one, can be an intimidating event. The eyes of strangers are penetrating; the eyes of familiar faces suddenly seem to look at you differently. It will take time to build relationships, to quiet the anxious voice inside that speaks your self-doubt. But what if, very soon in the integration process, you found someone with whom to form an alliance, someone with whom you felt safe, and someone who knew the ins and outs of what to you is a brave new world? Such a person, a mentor, would not only ease your anxiety by providing an outlet and resource but, as a guide, they would accelerate the process of integration so that you could get up to speed that much faster.

In the last century when a young man trained in one of the trades he joined a community that embodied much of what is described today as "the learning organization." Crude, tough, and brutal though the life of the apprentice may have been at times, the quality and consistency of the learning experience was never allowed to slip because the poor performance of one individual reflected on the community as a whole.

The young boy, legally bound by an apprenticeship or indentured agreement, was given over to the charge of a "master." (The boy's parents got the search fee.) The master clothed and fed the apprentice, and, in return, the apprentice worked for him. Although the early chores were menial, the boy had to learn the trade – to graduate, he had to produce a final piece of trade work, and this piece was judged by a standard that could never be anything less than excellent. Apprenticeship pieces reached such a high standard that in today's antique trade they often fetch very high prices.

A craftsman who excelled could move to the final stage of learning: he could become a master. But to reach that lofty pinnacle he had to produce a "masterpiece."

Although apprenticeship still exists in some of the trades, learning at the feet of the master has largely been replaced by a modularized system focusing on accelerated learning. Technology, organizational and production complexity, and the cost of training all made the shift inevitable and appropriate.

It can be argued that in breaking away from the master concept, and its tradition of work as an art form, we have lost something valuable. As if to emphasize that point, it is interesting to note that in England, crafts such as thatching and stonemasonry are making a serious comeback.

The modern incarnation of the apprenticeship process is mentoring. Mentoring has a great potential to impact the way less seasoned executives respond to change, challenge and opportunity.

Part of the problem with mentoring is that everybody seems to recognize its worth, but few seem to know how to make it work for them. It stands along side Jungian theories of personality, Emotional Intelligence, Neuro Linguistic Programming, and Action Learning as an invaluable yet untapped resource.

Complicating the problem further, mentoring is either confused with the coaching process, or seen as a form of formal counseling demanding, by implication, all of the skills and sensitivity of advanced therapeutic techniques.

But there is a clear difference between counseling, coaching, and mentoring; a difference perhaps best described in the following terms:

- **Counseling** addresses dysfunctional behavior of a personal nature.
- **Coaching** is exclusively about supporting employees in the quest to reach and maintain peak performance.
- **Mentoring** is about successful managers and/or executives sharing their experience with less-seasoned, high-performance employees - the result of mentoring is accelerated learning.

Organizations would be well advised to upgrade their mentoring capabilities for a number of reasons. It means higher employee retention; it results in meaningful dialogue that transcends the hierarchy of the organization; and, in an environment marked by global competitiveness, it makes for more effective learning.

But you're thinking, "I'm a big girl (or boy); I don't need to be dependent on some gray brow to tell me how they did it the Pleistocene era." "Hey, I was asked to take on this role; they must have seen something in me suggesting I could pull it off." This confidence will serve you well, but, sadly, it often doesn't last much past the first few days. The complexity of the tasks on hand, the need to learn and absorb an incredible amount of information in a short period of time, new ways to think, new language, and an immediate need to revisit long held views and opinions, all combine to shake and erode self-confidence.

Testimony from those who have successfully sailed the turbulent waters of integration suggests that nothing is more valuable than having someone trustworthy to talk to. The promoted or incoming executive will need someone who can explain the seemingly unexplainable, someone who can point out the political pitfalls, and someone who, if nothing else, can simply provide a sounding board off which you can safely bounce an idea that might have, in another context, exploded on impact.

What about the hiring executive? Here the water gets murky. Arguably, the individual best equipped to answer many of the questions the new executive might have would be the person to whom he or she reports. But what about safety; what about the anxiety of confessing ignorance of something to someone who might think you should know that already?

While, the hiring executive might be the most appropriate person to mentor given that he or she has the most to lose if the new executive stumbles, this needs to be approached with care and caution. The new executive's relationship with the hiring executive is extremely important. If it gets off on the wrong foot both the short and long-term consequences will be emotionally costly for all of the parties concerned. There will be questions that the new executive will not want to ask (diplomacy). Equally important, there will be elements of understanding that the hiring executive will be reluctant to provide. And finally, statistics suggest that very few executives have the skills and the know-how to truly support a new executive going through the trials and tribulations of trying to hit the ground running. But, this said, the hiring executive might just be the best person to steer the incoming executive toward an effective mentor.

A number of organizations have been wise enough to develop effective mentoring processes. Others have been enlightened enough to introduce a "buddy" system to support those who are going through the trauma of role shift. But these organizations are few and far between. What follows are suggestions and shared insights on how the new executive can reach out and ask for advice and support.

Finding a mentor

Care has to be taken when thinking about approaching a mentor. It is not just a matter of picking up the yellow pages and flipping to the "M"s.

In many instances it is advisable that the mentor not work for the organization. The value of independent counsel, uncomplicated by a dual relationship, cannot be overstated. The only downside is that he or she may not know enough about the organization and the new role to pose insightful questions. Choosing a mentor from within the organization can cause conflicts of interest. For obvious reasons, someone disappointed because he or she was not selected for the new role would probably not be a good choice. Equally, a new peer who is clearly a competitor for the next rung on the ladder should also be ruled out.

A good mentor is someone with integrity and a sense of personal balance. Success as a mentor comes only to those who view leadership through the aperture of serving. Effective mentors are not difficult to identify. They invariably display a quiet maturity. They are the sort of individuals who are constantly being brought into the confidence of others; they are regularly asked for advice.

Mentoring is ultimately about the chemistry of the relationship. It takes more than your admiration of their skills; your choice must be the kind of person who possesses the qualities, personal and professional, that encourage the two of you to "click." In a world of leadership scarcity, outstanding mentors are a golden asset. The best mentoring relationships don't flow, they sing. The best companies recognize this and reward mentors accordingly.

Reaching out

In an organization uncomfortable with the concept of mentoring, going outside of the organization is clearly a safe and often effective option. A good external mentor can be a previous colleague, a friend or a skilled consultant. In the case of a consultant, it is important that he or she have **extensive** business experience.

Much of what a mentor brings to the table is wisdom and judgement based on personal learning. If the person doesn't have the experience necessary, the advice you get will be theoretical rather than practical. The best internal mentoring relationships are those where the parties come together naturally. Forced marriages can work but often they don't.

Making the connection is far easier than most would think. Asking someone to provide mentoring is often received as a form of flattery. Now, drawing meaning from the relationship is obviously a challenge of a different order. Go slowly. Wait for that level of emotional comfort before confessing your deepest secret fears and confidences. Trust is the central element to a well-functioning mentor relationship.

Fit

Mentoring is not just a matter of finding someone you like – a nice person. In a world where the first year of an engineering program is out of date before the final year is completed, relevance of experience is a key consideration. Ideally, the mentor should have advanced at least **one** career development stage beyond

EXPERIENCE BASE / STAGES OF GROWTH	GENERAL MANAGER	TECHNICAL	SALES AND MARKETING	ADMIN.
LEARNING THE ROPES (20-27)	Building an understanding of the business landscape. Defining success. Establishing standards.			
FINDING ONE'S FEET (28-33)	Early management roles. A need to deal with failure. Important to build a range of management skills. Needs to see several business cycles from single role. International exposure invaluable.			
BUILDING SUCCESS (34-44)	Must establish track record. A time to move laterally. Move to roles with extended time horizons important. Exploring risk and being at the edge of comfort zone equips individual for later roles.			
MAKING EXPERIENCE COUNT (45-55)	Putting it all together. A time to know one's self. Lack of experience or lack of emotional maturity come back to derail. The contribution years.			
PASSING THE BATON (55+)	Life style and family come to the fore. Success termed more in the success of others. Asks the question: What did I contribute? Leaving a legacy and succession have a high priority.			

STAGES OF CAREER DEVELOPMENT

Figure 18

the individual being mentored. See **Figure 18**. Although many different mentoring relationships succeed, in a rapidly changing world currency of experience is lost quickly and approaching an internal mentor who has progressed two or more career stages beyond the new role requires modest caution. Note: this flies in the face of much that has historically been written about mentoring where "the mentor" is invariably described using the sort of terms one might use when talking about a favorite uncle.

In the traditional organization executives build their careers as if they were constructing a letter T. Only at the final stages of their careers, and in very senior roles, do they have responsibility that spans the total organization. If you have joined a business wedded to structure, rules and hierarchy the functional expertise of the mentor is clearly a critical factor. If on the other hand, the organization you have joined means that you have a number of different roles, roles that are anchored not in "the function" but in the process, and those roles cross cultural boundaries, then broad-based experience on the part of the mentor is desirable.

When choosing a mentor, the following rules of thumb are worth keeping in mind:

- In the "learning the ropes" career stage, a good mentor can come from anywhere in the organization. **See Figure 18**.

- At the "finding one's feet" stage the mentor should ideally have in-depth functional/technical expertise. If international experience is in the cards, the mentor should clearly be someone who has worked in the international arena.

- When "building success" involves a move into general management, or where the role spans the organization, the mentor should be someone whose expertise and experience is broad-based.

- As the executive moves into the later stages of his/her career interpersonal behavior, trust and maturity dominate considerations of fit.

The rules of engagement

Pre-nuptial agreements aside, the mentoring experience should start with a clear "contract" concerning the behavior of both parties. As a first step, both should agree on (1) the goals (outcomes) of the relationship, and, (2) the protocols that will guide the relationship. The acronym **LEARN** outlines a framework for these rules of process.

Let either side move away from the relationship with grace if either considers that little value is being added. No hard feelings clause.

Ensure that all discussion is balanced between dialogue (sharing experience) and exploring suggested actions. "I'm interested in your stories, but what are my options?" clause.

Agree on the timeframe for the integration support. "Are you still here?" clause.

Respect confidences at all cost. The vault clause.

No criticism of those whose names happen to come up during the discussion. The no judgements clause.

When the mentor is from within the organization the new executive must let his or her team leader know what's going on. This doesn't mean you need to compromise the confidentiality of the mentoring discussions, neither do you have to share the **specific** agenda of the discussions. But you do need to take care to ensure that you are not perceived as doing anything covert.

A good rule in the integration process, insofar as the immediate team leader is concerned is "no surprises." Indeed, in more traditional (T1) cultures, the need to "go through the established channels" is a dominant requirement. Even in Patron-style organizations that have a significant degree of empowerment, asking "permission" is an essential element of doing things "right."

Getting the mentoring relationship to the point where the new executive, the mentor and the hiring executive form a developmental triad is of tremendous benefit.

The five steps in a successful mentoring process

As with much in life the rule in mentoring is to keep it simple. A framework describing the key steps in a successful mentoring process is outlined in **Figure 19**.

Discussions with the mentor should begin (1) by defining the issue, problem, question, or opportunity. The most effective mentoring sessions are those where the agenda remains focused on one, possibly two, key issues. The ensuing dialogue should explore both the current situation and the desired state of things.

Time well spent in a mentoring discussion is time devoted to the next two steps: (2) reviewing options; and (3) sharing experience. The mentor's role in reviewing the options is less to come up with suggested ways to act than it is to challenge the new executive's mind set. By posing new questions the mentor can also stretch the new executive's imagination. By sharing his/her experience the mentor helps the new executive begin to understand where the pitfalls lie and how the opportunity can start to unfold. Although it's often helpful for the mentoring discussion to review the potential action steps, the mentor must make it clear that deciding on the course of action (4) lies with the new executive.

The mentoring discussion is not two executives coming together to decide what to do because mentoring is not, at its core, about problem solving. The mentor shares experience, poses new questions, and suggests where the holes in the road may lie — but he or she is an advisor not a partner in solving the problem(s). The mentor can provide invaluable input but he or she would be walking a tightrope if he/she did anything but remain a passive (but provocative) associate.

The mentor who intrudes into the decision-making arena is making a serious mistake Not only is he or she taking ownership for issues outside of his or her area of accountability, but, should things not unfold as planned, he or she might end up as the villain in the eyes of others.

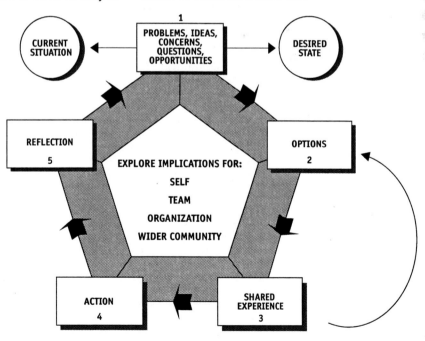

Figure 19

The mentor must also encourage the new executive to (5) spend time in reflection. Because time is the enemy of anyone moving into a new role, reflection is the one element of the integration process least likely to receive the necessary attention. The new executive must find time for reflection; must find time to process what it is she/he has learned; must create emotional and intellectual space such that new patterns of understanding can be interpreted and the meaning thought through. The mentor's role is to provoke and to encourage this kind of pointed reflection.

Suitable topics for the mentoring discussion

The kinds of topics suitable for a mentoring discussion are largely common sense. Clearly, however, some issues would be outside of an appropriate agenda — salary, compensation, bonus and benefits, behavior that may involve some form of disciplinary action, and disagreement between the hiring executive and the new executive over goals and/or priorities.

Topics that would be a natural fit within an effective mentoring process are all and any of the dimensions in the executive integration model that frames this book.

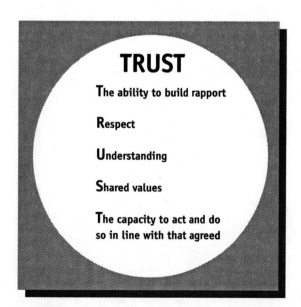

TRUST

The ability to build rapport

Respect

Understanding

Shared values

The capacity to act and do so in line with that agreed

Figure 20

Falling into the gray area of appropriateness are discussions that tend to be people related. Where the discussion touches on interpersonal issues, and especially where the discussion embraces the hiring executive, it is essential that the mentor not allow the dialogue to dwell on personal criticism of any of the parties involved.

Mentoring works best when the mentor is willing to share his or her own story

The mentor should be someone personally comfortable with, and possessing the language skills necessary to tell, his or her story. This, in particular, involves exploring times of failure, times of inadequate preparation, and times when the mentor could have made other key decisions.

The mentor's "story" lies at the heart of the mentoring experience. The mentor needs to be comfortable enough in him or herself to be willing to step back from his or her own experience and be dispassionately self-critical. Those entering the mentor role ready to recount only their successes are unlikely to add much value to the mentoring experience.

Trust is essential

The chemistry between the new executive and the mentor will only develop where there is a solid foundation of trust. Describing trust is about as tricky as one US Supreme Court Justice's attempt to describe pornography: "Although I can't define it, I sure know it when I see it." Having said that, there are five fundamental building blocks (**see Figure 20**) central to generating and maintaining a high level of trust:

1. The ability on the part of the mentor to quickly and easily build rapport; a capability for him or her to see the world through the eyes of the new executive; and a willingness to frame language, metaphor and experience in terms that the new executive can relate to.

2. The new executive must respect the mentor as someone who has "been there." If the mentor simply attempts to pontificate or draw meaning from a purely conceptual point of view - no matter how well crafted – he or she does little to build the respect demanded. For this reason, the most successful mentors are likely to be those who have "acted" on a stage where the script being played out was similar to the one now faced by the new executive.

3. The mentor must have the capacity to show empathetic understanding. Not only does this demand genuine listening skills, it means that the mentor must be an active listener. The mentor has to be able to listen not just to what is said, but also to what is **implied**.

4. The mentor and the new executive must operate from a set of common values. For example, if the mentor has an approach that is hierarchical and rooted in assumptions of command and control, he or she is unlikely to provide meaningful support to a new executive faced with the challenge of leadership in an environment dominated by self-managing teams. Similarly, a mentor whose experience has exclusively been in one culture is a poor fit with an executive who has an international role.

5. The act of mentoring demands a high level of personal commitment to the mentoring

process from both parties. Failure to fulfill that agreement is not only harmful to the mentor's relationship with the new executive (and vice versa), but it can have wider, negative implications for the way the new executive sees the overall organization. Similarly, to maintain a high level of trust, when the mentor and the new executive agree to take a course of action, they must do all in their power to deliver on that commitment.

The business community is aware of the need to build flexibility into any future market/customer scenario. The message: business success will depend as much on responsiveness as it will on the quality of the strategic thinking available. In response to these new demands, there has been a veritable avalanche of "solutions" hawked by management gurus, academics, consultants, training experts, and vicarious think tanks. Some of these remedies are invaluable tools in addressing organization effectiveness; others are destined to be less impactful.

There has been a similar deluge in new communication forms: the virtual office; teleconferencing; network organizational structures; management by e-mail; and other "advances" in the way we relate to each other. These forms, while offering instant access, do much to dehumanize the work place and in doing so erode a sense of community.

Not all the blame rests on the shoulders of technology. We can't underestimate the ways in which a global business climate of downsizing, rightsizing, organizational turbulence and lack of leadership have contributed to the general cynicism that lies somewhere to the center of this malaise. It is a malaise evidenced by erosion of loyalty, high employee turnover and lack of interest by the best business graduates when large organizations come a-calling.

Change, paradoxically, demands both the need to let go and the need for continuity. In the eye of a hurricane there is an area of calm. Mentoring reaches back to an ancient pattern of development, one that amid the hype of quick fixes, organizations have either forgotten about or overlooked. Ask virtually any successful executive and they will quickly link their success to the mentoring relationships they enjoyed along the way. Past organizational cultures built communities; they created ecosystems where mentoring flourished naturally. Today, that sense of common purpose and community needs to be rekindled.

The rate of change in our society makes speed of learning a critical dimension of competitive advantage. Mentoring, when conducted with professionalism and flair, can do much to accelerate talent through that learning curve. For the new executive, having someone to talk to isn't just useful, it's imperative. Mentoring may not be magic but it does have proven worth. And in an era of untested "solutions," it is an opportunity that the new executive would be wise to explore.

Chapter Six

Critical Learning

- Developing a mentoring relationship is an important part of building success in a new role.

- There is a significant difference between mentoring, coaching, and counseling.

- The choice of mentor depends on what stage of development the executive is at.

- The mentoring contract needs to include agreement of what is, and what is **not** part of the mentoring agenda.

- Mentoring works best when the mentor is prepared to share his/her own story.

- Trust is essential.

Consequences

An effective mentor shares his/her experience, poses new questions, and suggests where the holes in the road are. Working with a mentor not only ensures that the executive moves through the integration as quickly as possible, but can, when the mentoring relationship is well grounded, significantly enrich the overall learning experience. A new executive who ignores the value of an appropriate mentor is overlooking an invaluable resource.

Step back and reflect on the ideas that surfaced and the learning you take from this chapter. Consider the path you are on, the need to build relationships (fit), and your understanding of success in the new role (expectations). Think about what you need to stop doing, start doing, and that which you need to do differently.

_____

_____

_____

_____

_____

_____

_____

_____

_____

_____

_____

_____

Reaching agreement on the agenda

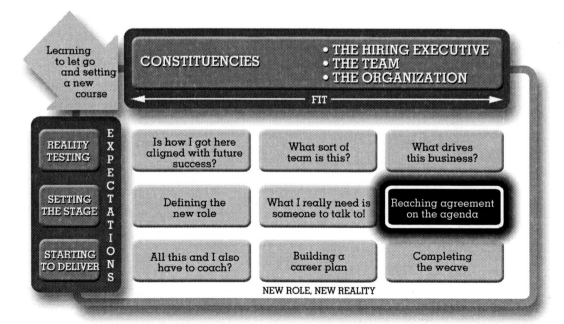

Reaching agreement on the agenda

A well-known scientist, describing his life's work, said "Behind apparent order lies chaos and yet deep within chaos lurks order." These words could equally describe the feelings of a promoted or incoming executive after just a few weeks in his or her new role.

When you first start a new role, you get the illusion of a meaningful structure underlying it. There seems to be a process, there seems to be order - this veil of comfort quickly parts, and behind it spin chaos and discord.

As the comfort recedes, it is replaced by frustration, disappointment, confusion and, above all else, a sense of being overwhelmed with the sheer volume of facts and information that have to be assimilated. More than likely, the cause of this was that the role was poorly defined, and the job specification — so lyrically described during the interview — is, in reality, little more than an embellished thumbnail sketch.

Unless the new executive is very fortunate the same will be true for his or her support throughout the integration period. After an exhilarating courtship and an all too brief honeymoon, it's into the kitchen to deal with the mountain of pots and pans that have piled up.

Although it may be poetically pleasing that a butterfly rubbing its hind feet together in a Borneo jungle can affect the weather in downtown Canton, Ohio, chaos in business is not an altogether desirable characteristic. The challenge for the executive in a new role is to find and define the order that lies behind the apparent turmoil. The new executive has to take account of all that he or she has learned up to this point, and start to find an area of calm in this otherwise stormy sea. The new executive must direct agreement concerning where the priorities lie.

It is **essential** that the new executive establish agreement (recontract) on his or her agenda

— both short- and long-term goals — early on in the new role. Even if the initial description of the role was comprehensive, in the time that has elapsed since the interview, priorities may well have changed, and new competitive forces may have emerged. Equally important, the executive him or herself now has a wealth of new information on which to act; he or she has looked at the quality of the new team, gained an understanding of what drives the business, and defined the role he or she is to play. So now, the promoted or incoming executive is, fledgling no more, in a real position to discuss with candor based on awareness, **what is and what isn't possible**.

Not being assertive in this regard means leaving the criteria for his or her success exclusively within the hands of others. In fact, unless there is agreement (a performance contract) about **specifically** what needs to be achieved, all manner of confusion will result. In developing and agreeing on the agenda there are a number of issues that the new executive should take into account.

Measure twice, cut once

Setting and agreeing on the agenda is a pivotal stage. Getting it wrong or holding back will almost certainly have repercussions later on at a time when the inaugural well of goodwill may have been used up. Before sitting down to discuss the agenda the prudent new executive needs to consider the following:

- Postponing this potentially difficult discussion with the hiring executive because of fear of conflict is self-defeating.

- In a world that is changing at an ever-increasing rate, past trends can be highly misleading.

- There is a significant difference between strategic thinking and strategic planning. The former is anchored in the belief that those dealing with a turbulent world must be willing to "paint outside of the lines." In that traditional strategic planning tends to follow a predetermined formula, it invariably limits both the opportunity for, and the quality of, strategic thinking. To break out of "the prison of structure" it is helpful that those charting the way forward (1) define the - four to six - most probable future scenarios and (2) ensure that the organization is agile enough to respond even if the least likely starts to unfold.

- A problem with any process or activity that attempts to "create tomorrow" is that teams get caught in "group think"; they are held captive by their common beliefs and assumptions. A team can compensate for this by inviting talented individuals from an entirely different field to regularly challenge their thinking. Group think is also less likely when one member of the team is asked to play the role of "maverick", an individual mandated to tell the team why the project they are passionately committed to won't work. After the debacle called the Bay of Pigs, President Kennedy insisted that at every cabinet meeting someone be appointed whose role it was to challenge the team's decisions. The person chosen: the individual most knowledgeable on the topic.

- Beware of the numbers game. An agenda that identifies issues such as revenue growth but fails to identify how the numbers will be achieved is like agreeing to win the Super Bowl and then asking: "Does anyone here have a football?"

- Waiting until hard information is available before acting isn't always necessary. The more complexity that gets overlaid on business problem solving and planning processes, the more traditional managers want the safety blanket of hard information. Opportunity, on the other hand, invariably means now! Tomorrow's successful executives will, of necessity, have a high regard for judgment, intuitive response, and comfort with ambiguity.

- To find a diamond one has to own a pick and a shovel. Setting the agenda should embrace not only the issues important to the organization but be reflective of the needs of **all** of the key stakeholders, the most critical stakeholder of all being the customer. Defining the customer's needs demands ongoing face-to-face contact.

- Most goal setting assumes an agenda of predictable change. The dilemma: the world is far from being predictable. Confronted by uncertainty the new executive can respond in one of two ways: (1) sit back and be buffeted by each new wave of change or (2) take steps to be the one that invents the future. The latter demands that at least one of the longer-term goals should involve an "unreasonable stretch." Unreasonable to the point that its achievement would only be possible if those charged with its accomplishment have to not only work, but think, differently.

Alignment means throwing a wide net and then pulling it tight

Immature executives often make the mistake of defining success purely in personal terms. By comparison, experienced leaders constantly seek ways to ensure that their contribution complements the work of others. Newcomers watch the road immediately front of them. A mature professional looks first to the horizon knowing that in doing so he/she is also taking the foreground into account. Before agreeing on the agenda, the new executive, in conjunction with his or her team, should consider the following questions:

- What actions would have the greatest impact on customer value?

- What are the performance goals of all of the other key stakeholders (e.g., shareholders)? What actions would have the greatest impact on the achievement of those goals?

- What is the one thing that the team can do to positively improve the end-to-end value chain? (e.g., driving out cost, improving working capital, working with customers and suppliers to create a greater degree of alignment)

- What targets does the hiring executive have?

- What priorities do others (e.g., other teams, the corporate office) who interface with the team have?

- What single barrier has historically prevented the team from reaching and sustaining the heights of success?

- What is the one thing the team can do to be more effective?

The new executive should establish no more than three to five clear priorities for the next 90 days. He/she should also establish a similar number of priorities for the balance of the financial or fiscal year. Remember, there should be at least one agenda item that extends more than one year out.

Agreeing on a "shopping list" of priorities not only makes it probable the new executive will take his or her "eye off the ball," but is likely to start raising questions about his/her ability to deliver. Each priority should meet the START criteria. **See Figure 21**.

As a word of caution, the promoted or incoming executive who sets an agenda without involving his or her team is making a mistake. Input is crucial. It doesn't have to mean absolute agreement - although agreement is invaluable - and it doesn't have to mean pandering to the whims, personal agenda, ego, or need for control of established team members. Without involvement there is no ownership. Without ownership there is no commitment. Without commitment little is possible.

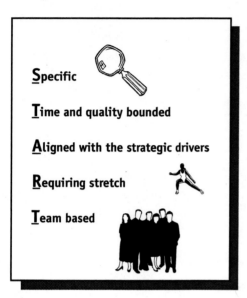

Specific

Time and quality bounded

Aligned with the strategic drivers

Requiring stretch

Team based

Figure 21

To get things done it is important to know how to manage upwards

Once the focus of the agenda is established, getting favorable, early agreement is really about knowing how to manage upwards. Though this concept might be alien to most business school classes, it is integral to the political savvy (and, thus, long-term survival) of any seasoned executive. A master class in managing-up would include the following advice:

- Know the hiring executive's hot buttons. Know the things that set him or her off.

- Build rapport by being an **attentive listener** - not just at the beginning but **always** - and by letting the hiring executive set the tone and the **pace** for meetings.

- Understand the hiring executive's personality type and work accordingly. If he or she is highly organized, get organized. If he or she is a stickler for detail, provide the detail. If he or she likes to start by framing the big picture, frame the big picture. If he or she is concerned about people, show how the team's actions will have a positive impact and on whom. If routine and repetition bore him or her, be adaptive, be creative, uncover a new card.

- Be prepared. **Always** be better prepared than the hiring executive when the topic is in your arena.

- Get to know the hiring executive's limitations - gently and respectfully provide support.

- **Never** make promises that can't be delivered on.

- Find out whom in the organization the hiring executive has the most difficulty with - gently and respectfully provide support.

- Find out what the hiring executive takes pride in. Be sure to never outdo him or her in that characteristic unless "permission" has been extended.

- If the hiring executive is outstanding at something, take advantage of that quality. You will not only make him or her feel good but you will also be using of all of the resources available - and that's the smart thing to do.

- Even in the world of empowerment and virtual organizations, make the hiring executive feel wanted. Keep him or her informed. Ask for help.

- Be honest, **but with timing and tact.**

- When things go well share the credit. If things come off the rails, accept the blame.

- **Never** criticize the hiring executive to others no matter how frustrating his or her actions may be.

- Let the hiring executive have the last word.

- Be humble.

- Be on time.

- Don't dress better than the hiring executive until you are in his/her role.

- Answer your E-mail.

- If the hiring executive is of the opposite sex, find a way to introduce him or her to your spouse as early as possible. If he or she is especially attractive do it sooner.

- Smile, but not **all** the time.

- Make sure everyone, including the cleaner and the person who fixes the Xerox machine, knows how to contact you.

- Never, never, never, make the hiring executive look bad in front of others - or anywhere else for that matter - because it breaks the golden rule: no matter what the circumstances, "**make the hiring executive look good.**"

- If you intend to give negative feedback, think about it for at least a year before making your move.

- Don't accept a golf or squash invitation unless you know how to play. If ahead, don't win by much.

- If any of the above impinge on your integrity or in a serious way start chipping away at your self-esteem, become a hermit.

Delegation ain't what it used to be

The traditional mind-set around delegation is that tasks that take up a lot of time and/or are repetitive are the first things the supervisor passes to his or her subordinates. The rationale: pawning off the grunt work gives the supervisor more time to do important "thinking" work. The logic: the higher in the organization you are, the more valuable you become.

A more enlightened approach understands delegation not as a technique to make the supervisor's job less annoying, but as a strategy that develops trust, succession and learning. In organizations where hierarchy is dramatically flattened and where knowledge becomes the basis of competitiveness, the rationale that governs delegation is not what makes the leader's job easier but what's effective. But this said, the ultimate decision when it comes to strategy, performance feedback, recruitment, and discipline must remain the prerogative of the leader.

Leadership is about turning the agenda into action

The inherent value in agreeing on the agenda is that it pinpoints **what needs to change**. The agenda is not, however, a suggested way to move forward that regresses shortly after consensus. To be worth the value of the paper it is printed on, it must be a **commitment to act**, and it is not fully functional as an agenda **until something happens**.

Stepping back to think about change is an important prelude to any agenda-setting discussion. *It is always useful to have a basic understanding of how a car works before attempting to fix it!* By the same token, an agenda that merely describes a set of intended actions without thinking through **how** they are to be enacted is a recipe for continuity and mediocrity.

Even the most hardy bushes and plants will not flourish in ground that is not receptive. In enacting the new agenda, the new executive has to do more than just communicate what is desired. He or she has to break established patterns of thought, find ways to challenge the status quo and recalibrate tension in the organization.

For this to happen, the agenda, once agreed upon, must move beyond the new executive and the hiring executive and engage the new executive's subordinate team and, beyond that, other key employees. A successful change agenda appeals to the head, the hand, the heart, and the spirit.

Feedback, feedback, feedback

A congressman from the deep South once said that the secret to his success lay in the fact that his supporters voted early and voted often. This could well be an appropriate anthem for the promoted or incoming executive: get feedback early and get it often. Feedback is not only important as a kind of behavioral compass, to reassure the new executive that he or she is on track, it is also an important part of building rapport.

When looking to encourage productive feedback, consider the following guidelines:

- There should be a feedback session with the hiring executive at least once a quarter during the first 12 months. These need not be highly formal sessions but neither should they be a quick "so how am I doing?"

- Make it easy for the hiring executive: the feedback session should be led by the new executive and should take the hiring executive through progress measured against the agreed agenda. And the session should embrace what it is that the new executive **is doing** to achieve the agreed results. Discussing the "how" lets the hiring executive suggest ways to overcome roadblocks and avoid pitfalls. The alternative is waiting until the year-end, or waiting to get called in because of a problem or concern that the hiring executive has heard about. Waiting carries with it a potentially high opportunity cost. If the basis of dialogue is response to problems, the hiring executive ends up forced into the role of performance policeman (and you are put on the defensive as the accused). Not the most meaningful way to build trust.

- Between six and nine months into the role the incoming or promoted executive should explore the value of 360° feedback. There are two important considerations here: (1) the net should be thrown wide and include customers and other key stakeholders; (2) the competencies upon which the 360° review is based should be **specific** to the new role. Care should be taken with the final point, in particular. Developing a role-specific competency profile and developing the 360° questionnaire is a time-consuming activity. But if the process is well designed, the time spent is more than balanced by the value of the resulting information. In some circumstances, consideration should be given to a 360°

review based not on a questionnaire but on personal interviews. An external consultant best facilitates such an approach. A series of personal interviews has the advantage of allowing the consultant to ask follow-up questions and generally dig deeper.

- The promoted or incoming executive impacts the work pattern of a good many people. For those who report directly to him or her, the new relationship can be especially stressful. They are wondering: have the rules changed? Do I need to work differently to succeed? Is my style congruent with my new manager's expectations? How much freedom do I have to make decisions? What support can I expect? To what extent are my personal career expectations going to be furthered or handicapped by this new player? Getting your team involved in setting the agenda will quiet some of these anxieties, but, for the most part, removing fear and developing trust will be an ongoing process. Addressing these concerns has to be part of the coaching process and it has to be based on early and regular feedback.

In AD 66, Petronius Arbiter wrote: "We trained hard... but every time we were beginning to form up teams, we would be reorganized. I was to learn later in life that we tend to meet any new situation by reorganizing... and a wonderful method it can be for creating the illusion of progress while producing inefficiency and demoralization."

Although written almost two thousand years ago, Petronious' words affirm the danger and challenge of moving into a new role. New executives rightly see their role as being to reorganize, to redraw the playbook and bring a new sense of order and energy to the role. What they often fail to recognize is that he or she needs a sense of focus and involvement in charting the new direction. He or she must encourage early feedback, engage the front-line "troops," and energize the patterns of play, or his or her new team can quickly become as disillusioned as Petronious.

Chapter Seven

Critical Learning

- Establishing the performance contract is an imperative.

- At least one of the agreed goals should be "unreasonable."

- The goals should take into account the role and priorities of others.

- There should be no more than 3 to 5 priorities.

- Part of the managing performance is to know how to manage upwards.

- Delegation should engender learning.

- The goals have to be turned into action.

- Agreeing on the timing and process for feedback is essential.

Consequences

Defining the role outlines the area of contribution. It sets out the playing field. Now the new executive and the boss must agree on what the score should be. The new executive who doesn't do this early on is setting him/herself up for a fall. Without agreement on specifically what needs to be achieved, it is literally impossible for the new executive to be successful.

Step back and reflect on the ideas that surfaced and the learning you take from this chapter. Consider the path you are on, the need to build relationships (fit), and your understanding of success in the new role (expectations). Think about what you need to stop doing, start doing, and that which you need to do differently.

_____

_____

_____

_____

_____

_____

_____

_____

_____

_____

All this and I also have to coach?

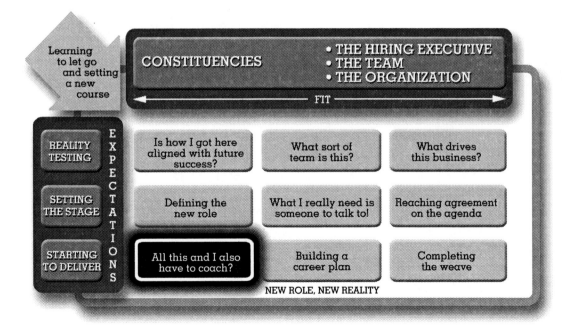

All this and I also have to coach?

Experience reveals that the challenge of a new role is likely to move the executive to the very edge of his/her comfort zone. One could argue that this is merely the price to be paid for what is a rich, and for many, an invaluable learning experience. The response: an undeniable temptation when "chaos" reigns to look for stability. For someone moving into a new role, this need for control is especially attractive. Would it not, therefore, be prudent for the new executive to put coaching off until he/she understands the lay of the land better? Why rock the boat? Why not see how things play out and then act? The dilemma: an executive who wants to thrive in an "unknown" environment cannot afford to wait and hope that the team he/she has inherited will somehow, magically, deliver the results demanded.

Putting coaching off presumes that coaching is a tangential or secondary element of the leadership process. Nothing could be further from the truth. Successful leaders are masters in the art of change. A leader who wants to make a difference must be prepared to challenge the status quo, disrupt established patterns of behavior, and introduce new skills. That being said, creating "a new way to be" is not the act of a solo performer; to lead is to take the team where they otherwise would not go. To make that journey a reality is to coach!

Coaching is the secret weapon of outstanding leaders. There is only so much that a business can productively do by way of downsizing, restructuring, focusing on the core business and such. Ultimately, it comes down to people - building teams that want to win and do win!

It is difficult, even for those on the cutting edge of technology, to appreciate how quickly the world is changing. As a species we are programmed to respond to major shifts or life-threatening events. But discontinuities, when masked by rapid-fire incremental changes occurring over a long period of time, lose much of their emotional impact. Few become aware that their skills have become redundant. To be successful the new executive has to think and act as if the competition is about to change the game. And guess what: they are!

All this and I
also have to
coach?

In 1903 Harry Andrews, the British Olympic Coach, stated with certain finality that "The mile record is 4 minutes 12.75 seconds. This record will never be broken." For those that listened (and believed), his words were, of course, prophetically true. Many medical experts perceived breaking four minutes as beyond human capability. When Roger Bannister ran 3 minutes 59.4 on a blustery day at Oxford in 1954, he was doing more than breaking records; he was redefining what was believed to be possible. What is informative about Bannister's feat is that following his breaking through the emotional barrier of four minutes, the sub-four minute mile was to become commonplace.

Like Bannister, the successful new executive is challenged to redefine what is possible, thinking drawn not out of past practice but out of courage, character, and an ability to compete for people's dreams.

The promoted or incoming executive must view leadership as moving beyond "managing what is" — a quest that is possible **only** if the new executive is prepared to disassemble unnecessary hierarchy, and lead through a "serving" mind-set. To make this a reality, the role of COP (Coerce, Organize, Punish) has to give way to the role of CHEERleader (CHallenge, Empower, Encourage, Reinforce). It is a transition ultimately dependent upon the ability of the new executive to coach.

The traditional hierarchical organization was built around the assumption that the employee was secondary to the technology – he or she was, at best, an extension of the machine. Today, in that ideas dominate, human capital becomes not only an organization's most valuable asset, but, in many respects, its only truly differentiating resource. Failure to nurture that resource, failure to invest in processes such as coaching, is no less shortsighted than attempting to compete using yesterday's equipment.

For most of those moving into a new role, coaching is either something they believe they do well, or a leadership competency that they know they should be better at. Even those that excel, however, often lack the insight necessary to define and evaluate why they are successful as a coach. They make a difference but have little or no ability to share what it is they do with others. For the new executive it is not enough that she/he be an exemplary coach, to excel she/he must also build mastery in coaching others in how to coach.

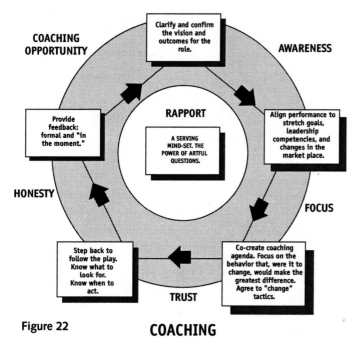

COACHING OPPORTUNITY

Clarify and confirm the vision and outcomes for the role.

AWARENESS

Provide feedback: formal and "in the moment."

RAPPORT

A SERVING MIND-SET. THE POWER OF ARTFUL QUESTIONS.

Align performance to stretch goals, leadership competencies, and changes in the market place.

HONESTY

FOCUS

Step back to follow the play. Know what to look for. Know when to act.

Co-create coaching agenda. Focus on the behavior that, were it to change, would make the greatest difference. Agree to "change" tactics.

TRUST

Figure 22

COACHING

For coaching to become a systemic and sustaining way for the organization to do business, a coaching philosophy must be supported by the freedom to act, access to information, a sense of optimism, a willingness to learn from mistakes, an openness to risk, and a belief that the organization is a learning community. Put simply, effective and meaningful coaching is difficult to sustain in a head and hand culture. A master coach balances the head (what), the hand (how), the heart (why), and spirit (who gains).

Coaching, to be successful, must be an extension of the leadership philosophy within the business. Where there is a well-articulated leadership philosophy, alignment becomes an imperative. A critical part of the coaching role is thus to enunciate this philosophy, to act out what it means and build alignment by "joining the dots" between mission, vision, values, business processes, opportunity, goals, behavior and feedback.

What follows are a series of insights - both conceptual and practical - that define that elusive, subtle, yet all-so-important characteristic of executive integration success: knowing how to coach. The ideas provide a framework for action that will add value even for those who would describe themselves as being a "master coach." **See Figure 22.**

A serving mind-set

Coaching is, exclusively, a process focusing on enhanced performance. Coaching should not be confused with counseling or mentoring. The former addresses the employee's dysfunctional emotional state. The latter is a means whereby a seasoned colleague shares his or her experience in order to "fast track" the career growth of a less seasoned, high potential, employee.

Chapter 8

*All this and I
also have to
coach?*

Coaching is a deep-rooted managerial philosophy, not a periodic activity. As such, coaching is a more evolved and proactive form of leadership than that typical of command and control management. The most apparent difference is that employees working with a talented coach play to win and not to avoid failure.

The emotional genesis of the coaching process must be the employee's needs - not those of the coach. To be a master coach demands a level of maturity, and a willingness to submerge ego that few managers attain. Those who enjoy the greatest degree of success as a coach see coaching as a privilege and not an onerous task. A master coach operates out of a **serving mind-set**.

A serving mind-set is apparent not only in the way the coach approaches those within his/her span of influence but in the coach's perception of self. A master coach constantly pushes him/herself to the edge of his/her own comfort zone, seeks feedback, admits when he/she is wrong, and is open to coaching from others.

A coach who truly makes a difference does so not for personal gain but out of an authentic sense of caring. A master coach cares enough to initiate tough conversations, cares enough to share what he/she feels and cares enough to always find time to coach. A coach who cares touches the heart and enriches the spirit of those that he/she works with.

Because at least half of all communication is non-verbal, an important dimension of coaching success is what the new executive believes, and non-verbally communicates, is possible. Similarly, what the new executive does before and after the coaching discussion is far more important than anything he or she might say during it. This ability to build and maintain **rapport** is the hallmark of a master coach. Rapport finds its outlet in every facet of the coaching experience. Affirmation, reinforcing success, and positive feedback for example may well be best delivered with a simple nod, a smile, or positive body language.

Meaningful coaching and **focus** are synonymous. Success in coaching is achieved when the agenda for change focuses on one aspect of behavior at a time.

Central to the coaching process are **trust,** mutual respect, common purpose, integrity, openness, and **honesty**. A leader who does not engender trust cannot coach. A leader who deals in half-truths and/or who slants the truth to his/her own purpose will never rise above the level of mediocrity.

Coaching can and does take many forms, but these are the two most common: (1) a planned, formal coaching session; and (2) an unplanned/intuitive response to a dilemma, opportunity and/or success. The theme underlying all successful coaching is "heightened employee self-awareness." Many of the best opportunities for such directed insight happen "in the moment." In such instances, because the intervention is unplanned and the coaching spontaneous, the feedback is often highly impactful.

Although the outcome of meaningful coaching is enhanced performance, the genesis of any lasting change must rest in *balance* between head, hand, heart and spirit. For the head: identify the change that needs to take place. For the hand: determine how the change is to be realized. For the heart: determine the value to the employee. And, for the spirit, define how this change will enrich the employee's life beyond the immediate role. *Balance* is best described by the belief that quality of life flows from expressing oneself through work, not existing for one's work.

Not all employees can be or want to be coached. Coaching is best aimed at those already operating at a successful level of performance, having the potential to stretch. Coaching is about drawing out latent potential and building positive commitment, not mending those that are "broken."

Clarify the vision and explore outcomes for the role

The new executive must be highly attuned to the context within which the coaching opportunity arises. A leader who delegates to a lower level of importance the needs of the other stakeholders in the coaching process is charting a dangerous course. The value and speed of action needed to meet the customer's expectations must, in particular, always be to the fore. Sensitivity to the context can be seen in the way the coach takes account of the history of change within the business, the philosophy within the enterprise towards learning and leadership, and the extent to which the organization offers appropriate role models.

*All this and I
also have to
coach?*

Before discussing the vision and desired outcomes, there must be agreement about the underlying mission for the organization, business unit and/or team: Why are we here?

The higher the seas and the faster the current, the more those sailing on them need a working compass. In the same way, the more confusing the marketplace and the more diverse the culture, the more those negotiating the change need an overarching sense of direction. Without a defining mission, other elements of the coaching process exist in a vacuum. The mission provides direction; the mission becomes the calm in the center of a storm. The mission becomes the reason to be.

A meaningful and effective first step in the coaching relationship is for the promoted and incoming executive to share (clarify) his or her vision of what future success looks, sounds and feels like. However, before he or she can build commitment and enthusiasm around the vision, several fundamental building blocks must be in place:

• The new executive has to have a fully formed picture of what future success looks like.

• He or she must describe the vision using language (examples, imagery, and metaphors) drawn from the employee's background, knowledge, and experience.

• The picture must be specific enough for the incoming or promoted executive to be able to compare actual behavior with his or her vision – from these comparisons, the executive can orchestrate insightful and appropriate coaching interventions.

• The incoming or promoted executive must, through his or her overt behavior, present an emotional commitment to the vision.

• The new executive must be willing to reexamine his or her perception of the vision based on input from the team. This does not mean that the final vision is, of necessity, a process dependent upon consensus. That being said, for there to be emotional buy-in, the vision must hold meaning for **all** of those involved.

In a world marked by speed of action, ambiguity, and a need for innovation, empowered behavior is guided by a set of personal and organizational values that must be held in common. If the coach's own behavior is not congruent with these espoused values, coaching becomes a manipulative process based on coercion rather that cooperation.

Enunciating the vision leads naturally to a conversation focusing on what **the employee** believes are the quantitative and qualitative outcomes for the role. In discussing how the employee defines qualitative success the coach should pose artful questions that surface:

- The perceived behavior(s) assumed to create optimum value for the customer.

- The employee's perception of his/her performance.

- Where the employee believes he/she can make the greatest difference.

Aligning performance to the stretch goals, leadership competencies and changes in the market place

It is highly unlikely that extraordinary performance will result from expectations built out of past practice. At least one of the agreed quantitative outcomes should be "audacious" – it must promote a high level of s t r e t c h . An audacious goal encourages people to dream, forces people to touch what they are truly capable of and releases untapped potential. An audacious goal compels the employee to not only revisit assumptions about the challenge on hand but reinvent what is possible. An audacious goal is non-negotiable.

Whilst contracting performance expectations, the coach must be ever conscious of the following questions:

- Does the employee have a robust understanding of his/her role? Does the employee's perception of the role balance head, hand, heart and spirit?

- Does the employee have a rich understanding of the core business process(es) he/she makes a contribution to? Does the employee understand the implication of his/her work to the overall value chain? Does the employee understand the synergy/interrelationship between the core business processes?

- Is the way forward, as outlined by the employee, aligned with the organization's "non-negotiable" leadership competencies? Is the way forward aligned with any specific competencies for the role in question?

- Are there opportunities for personal and performance growth that the employee has either not recognized or failed to capitalize on?

- Recognizing that aggressive stretch goals demand commitment and courage, does the employee also have access to the learning resources needed - theory, concepts, mentoring, best practice, training, pooled knowledge?

Any discussion on alignment should address the scope the employee has to make independent decisions, and in what situations the team or team leader needs to become involved. The range of freedom should be based upon the experience and competency of the employee in conjunction with the philosophy within the organization regarding employee involvement.

A master coach has a highly tuned understanding of when to **stop coaching** - when to allow the team the space to stretch and reach for their potential. With a great team, the group's needs are often best served when the coach moves into the role of advisor. An advisor is drawn into the fray at the request of the team or individual team member.

It is important that the new executive dispel the notion that an organization that emphasizes coaching makes **all** decisions by consensus. Some decisions, especially those that will unfold over a long time and those that have a sweeping impact on the total organization, can only be made by those in top leadership roles.

Co-creating the coaching agenda

The coaching agenda is the product of a conversation drawn out of a simple question: "If you were achieving the stretch goals, what would you be doing that you are not doing now?" Co-creating the coaching agenda has but one simple objective: to agree on changes to the employee's behavior that, if implemented, would have the optimum impact on the employee's performance.

Beginnings start with endings. For that reason a successful coaching agenda should also encompass what it is the employee should stop doing, or what limiting mind-sets the employee needs to let go of or reframe.

True learning results in personal change. Learning that results in change cannot come exclusively from books, case studies, simulations, practice, interactive multi-media support, meditation, or any of the other invaluable learning aids. Lasting change is rooted in **action**. Thus, the outcome of a meaningful coaching agenda must be a change in **the way the employee actually does the work**.

The greatest limitation to coaching success lies with what the employee believes is possible. Employee negative self-talk is the greatest challenge the coach will face – finding a way to deal with the self-limiting internal dialogue is key to coaching success. To build affirming self-talk, the coach must encourage the employee to use self-fulfilling statements when describing future performance e.g. "we will" and not "we will try." To engender optimism, the master coach also provides positive reinforcement of even small, initial steps.

The coaching agenda needs to address change pragmatically. Where the problem lies at the level of mind-set or beliefs, training will be of only marginal value. Similarly, not a few employees are simply in the wrong role. Attempts to coach an employee who is not suited to the role is something like teaching an elephant to dance: there is little chance of success and eventually both of the parties involved are destined to get very upset. When coaching has been carried through with purpose, subtlety, and character, but the behavior remains unchanged, it is logical to conclude that the employee is in the wrong role.

We all fall into and follow established paths. Patterns of thinking give us a sense of comfort (often misplaced) that the world is unfolding in a way that we can relate to. Established ways to act, experience, language, and beliefs, combine to allow us to make sense of the world. The most precious thing that a coach can achieve is to enable the employee to see the world from a different perspective, to view an emerging opportunity and/or problem with a new set of eyes. To create a shift of this kind the coach needs to consider the extent to which his or her own behavior impacts on the employee. A master coach understands the power of metaphors, the merit of exploring best practice, the value of changing the patterns of play, and introducing questions that challenge the status quo.

Employees excel when they take a sense of joy in the work they do. Passion is the untapped resource in all of us. Helping the employee find this sense of emotional oneness with the task is the ultimate goal of every master coach. In doing so the coach is not only serving the individual in terms of his or her organizational potential, but is releasing resources from which the employee can draw a richness of spirit that will impact every facet of his or her life.

Chapter 8

*All this and I
also have to
coach?*

The coach, probing for how the employee *could* act differently, makes it more likely that the employee *will* act differently if he or she:

- Asks those displaying the language or posture of failure to run through a mental video of at least one successful future scenario: imagery that allows the employee to live tomorrow's success today.

- Helps the employee consciously listen to the "sound" of future success. What are people saying?

- Helps the employee to understand that meaningful learning is invariably an uncomfortable experience.

- Helps the employee identify that which he/she needs to let go of.

- Recognizes that those who have the most to lose are those who will work the hardest to retain the status quo.

- Links positive outcomes to what the employee cares about most.

The coach should bear in mind that all learning starts with a question. One insightful question is worth many hours of telling the employee "how to." The coach, however, should avoid posing questions that he or she already appears to have an answer for. Failure to live by this rule will make the coach appear manipulative and lacking in integrity.

The single most important question the coach can ask is: What can I do differently? When the coach asks the employee what he/she (the coach) should do differently to enhance the employee's performance, the coaching experience becomes a shared journey of learning and self-discovery.

It is important that early on in the coaching relationship, ownership of the problem or opportunity passes to the employee. For this reason language such as, "Here is what I would like you to do," should be replaced by, "How would you like to address this?"

A master coach is a master storyteller. A rich story addresses the head, enables the hand, engages the heart and enriches the spirit. The best stories are those drawn from the organization that describe leadership in the face of adversity. That does not mean that stories need always be about successful ventures. Organizations that encourage risk tell stories about how people who fail – in pursuit of the organization's vision – are rewarded. A story delivered from the heart taps into a source of mental energy that is difficult to access in any other way. The best stories give those listening the courage to see the world differently. When people tell a story about themselves they are sharing who they are. A master coach in listening to the employee's "story" is gaining a unique insight into the employee's assumptions, beliefs and sense of identity.

The coach must get the employee's commitment, external and internal, to any agreed change of behavior. Ownership of the new behavior should reside with the employee. Success is dramatically increased when the employee defines where the opportunity lies and the process to bring about change.

Any agreed action steps should emphasize:

- The employee's learning style. Each of us learns faster when the coach introduces a challenge or opportunity by emphasizing one of the following: (1) interaction and dis-cussion about what's involved; (2) a conceptual model that draws together all of the component pieces; (3) watching, modeling, and, through reflection, building on the success of others; and, (4) exploration — learning through action and then exploring what happened.

- That traditional classroom training is an inadequate substitute for situational learning focusing on a real problem.

- The ongoing need to measure the performance improvement.

Stepping back to follow the play

Having agreed on the coaching agenda, the new executive must step back and give the employee the opportunity to deliver. For the new executive this involves a degree of risk, and for the employee used to having someone to fall back on it can appear like abandonment. Stepping back does not mean that the coach ignores the actions of the employee. The master coach is always aware of what is happening on the field and will use "time outs" judiciously and with subtlety to give feedback or pose a new question.

The coach must understand that before the employee can change four conditions must be met:

- The employee must *know* what to change.
- There must be the *will* to change.
- The employee must have the *capability* to act in the way agreed upon.
- The employee must be given the *opportunity* to practice the new behavior.

Creating opportunity is often the most difficult condition to foster because it means the coach has to first trust the players and then get out of the way.

One of the most important contributions a coach can make is to encourage the employee to **act**. Unfortunately, complexity and the emotional challenge of transformational change have created a business culture that has made many of the "survivors" skilled in the art of "risk avoidance." A workplace that limits risk is one that limits people's capacity to learn. Equally important, the ability to overcome risk is an essential ingredient in building self-confidence and self-esteem.

Self-affirming **action** is rooted in a constant striving for excellence. The dilemma: the quest for excellence is an ever-flowing river, ever-changing and subject to high and low water marks. And, like a river, what's happening on the surface isn't necessarily a good indication of what is happening below. A master coach is ever mindful of the ebb and flow of performance, and knows what debris or which log needs to be drawn out first in the event of a logjam.

The "glue" that holds the elements of the coaching process together is **shared awareness**. For the employee, it is awareness concerning the impact his or her behavior is having on others in the organization. For the coach, it is awareness of the world of the employee. Awareness of this kind requires both attention to the moment, and the capacity to have the employee interpret his/her behavior as if he/she were sitting in the audience watching a play. At the same time, all the players must be made aware that a successful play has three acts: (Act 1) insight into how an unfolding past has created today; (Act 2) the capacity to focus on that which is truly important; and (Act 3), the wisdom to link today's actions with tomorrow's reality.

Effective learning takes place **at the limit of what an employee believes is possible**. Pushing the employee to move beyond this *edge* - and in doing so generating emotional fear - does little for the organization and even less for the growth and self-confidence of the individual.

An invaluable form of coaching occurs when team members coach each other. Before this can happen several elements need to be brought together:

• Team members need to be coached in how to coach.

• Openness has to be a feature of team behavior.

• The team needs to have reached a level of maturity such that shared accountability, mutuality of goals, trust, and a high degree of interdependability are present.

Giving feedback

The master coach is always acutely aware that in building self-esteem, timing is everything.

Two forms of feedback dominate the coaching process: feedback that looks back over an extended period, and "in the moment" feedback intended as a springboard to future behavior. The former is a critical dimension of performance management. If delivered with honesty and respect it can be the one component of the formal performance review that has lasting value. Having said that, it loses much of its impact if it is part of a process whose "rating" system uses such confidence-sapping terms such as "average" or "competent." Or, even worse, a numerical score. If at least 80% of those "reviewed" cannot be adjudged "successful," the new executive would be well advised to challenge the assumptions upon which the performance management process is based.

One of the most powerful techniques that a coach can access is "silence." An artful pause engenders reflection. The space that surrounds a core question adds to its poignancy. A frame around the picture that describes tomorrow's success makes the image more vibrant. Bringing an appropriate level of drama to feedback will ensure that it is perceived to have emotional veracity.

An early dilemma for the coach is sorting out whether a performance shortfall is a "can't do problem" or a "won't do" problem. "Won't do" issues, because they often reflect deep-rooted attitude problems, are best addressed through counseling.

*All this and I
also have to
coach?*

A coach who presents feedback as if it were the absolute and undeniable truth, builds resentment and erodes respect. Omnipotence does little to set the context for meaningful dialogue. To avoid the illusion of being "absolutely" right, the coach should acknowledge up front that any direct feedback is nothing more than the coach's interpretation of events. For this reason, feedback should be presented along the lines of - "as I see it." To support this sense of joint review, "you should" structures are better framed as "I think." The integrity of this process will be supported and meaningful dialogue encouraged if the employee knows it is healthy to disagree with the input.

Where the focus of the coaching discussion is a problem to be resolved, the coach is ill advised to start the coaching discussion with overt praise or an outline of the employee's strengths. The resulting "but" transition will negate the positive elements of the discussion and make it highly unlikely that the employee will listen to future positive reinforcement without waiting for the other shoe to drop.

If there is no follow-up, little will change. A high value follow-up tactic is to "catch 'em doing it right."

Even where the focus is praise, one of the most performance limiting things a coach can do is to use "meta-language" e.g. "you did a great job." Praise that does not focus on the specific behavior involved blurs the good with the not so good and in doing so strips the feedback of any meaning.

The coach should not be reticent in offering what he or she believes to be possible remedies to performance difficulties. Presenting possible options is very different from **telling** the employee how he or she should act. Suggestions and input should complement, not limit or be a substitute for, insightful questions.

Negative feedback is most valuable when it is delivered with honesty and sensitivity, and when it is drawn from more than one source. Input from the customer is especially impactful. Negative feedback should question the result, process, tactics, or strategy, but never the personal qualities of the individual.

Time, place, and interpersonal rapport are variables that significantly impact the effectiveness of feedback. Negative feedback should always be followed shortly thereafter by an opportunity to correct the behavior in question. Allowing the employee to dwell on the criticism or problem has the effect of imprinting failure in the mind of the employee and thus makes it more likely, not less, that the problem will recur.

It is not the role of the coach to motivate the employee but to set the context so that, with encouragement and development, the employee can reach his or her full potential. A master coach is aware that some people are naturally drawn to future success while others change only when staying where they are becomes an unpalatable option. Behavioral change is best achieved where there is a sensitive balance between building self-esteem, and introducing creative tension. Therefore, dialogue (feedback) between the coach and the employee should cover an honest appraisal of the consequences of not adopting the agreed new behavior.

Finding the time to celebrate success is central to the coaching process. The celebration can be formal or informal, elaborate or simple. Celebration provides the employee an opportunity to both recharge his/her batteries and reaffirm the worth of the work being undertaken.

* * * * *

Organizations that survive and thrive in the years ahead are going to be entirely different from those that made their name when the world was stable and where the rate of change was, relatively speaking, manageable. To adapt to an environment marked by turbulence means that the new executive will have to create value from, and through, **all** of his or her resources.

The leader who remained at the helm because he or she exercised power through a combination of position and access is a thing of the past. For organizations and front-line leaders alike, the transition from **boss** (power over) to **facilitator** (power with), from facilitator to **coach** (power to), and, in some instances, from coach to **advisor** (power from) is already well advanced. The spirit of coaching is with us; however, still lacking are the skills to deliver on good intent. The promoted or incoming executive who explores, discovers and develops these skills will find him or herself a secure place among a group of players truly defined as being "masterful."

Chapter Eight

Critical Learning

- Successful leaders are masters in the art of change.

- Coaching is a way to be.

- Coaching is about drawing out latent potential and building positive commitment – not mending those that are broken.

- Coaching starts with a clear vision.

- Goals have to be aligned with the leadership competencies and changes in the marketplace.

- The coaching agenda should be co-created.

- A master coach knows when to step back and follow the play.

- Giving feedback is an art form unto itself.

Consequences

A leader who doesn't coach, or one who thinks that it is something that can be delegated, is not creating optimum value out of the resources he/she has been given stewardship of. To lead is to bring about change. Change ultimately means that people have to change. Not to coach is thus to turn one's back on a competency that is a fundamental part of being a successful leader.

*All this and I
also have to
coach?*

Step back and reflect on the ideas that surfaced and the learning you take from this chapter. Consider the path you are on, the need to build relationships (fit), and your understanding of success in the new role (expectations). Think about what you need to stop doing, start doing, and that which you need to do differently.

_____

_____

_____

_____

_____

_____

_____

_____

_____

_____

_____

_____

_____

Chapter nine

Building a career plan

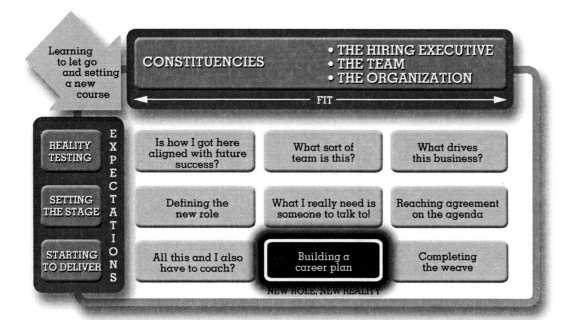

Building a career plan

For the promoted, newly hired, or those faced with a new way to work, the journey is a cocktail of challenge, exhilaration, trepidation, fear, surprise, stress and, not to be forgotten, hard work. Some move into a new role and find their feet relatively quickly. Others make progress but discover that their reserves of emotional energy get so depleted that what seemed an exciting challenge has lost much of its appeal. Still others stumble during those first few important weeks and make an early decision that the new role isn't right for them.

The difference between those who hit the ground running and those who struggle can often be accounted for in relatively simple ways: a colleague who is prepared to go out of his or her way to offer support; a mentor who knows where the pitfalls lie; an executive search consultant who follows through; and a hiring executive who is supportive. Climbing a mountain is clearly a lot easier if you're trained to cope with the terrain, if you've been given the right tools and the know-how to work as part of a team.

For those so equipped, moving into a new role can be a rite of passage, a labor of love, an accelerated learning experience that transcends anything offered within the hallowed walls of an MBA-granting institution. The investment needed to turn frustration into a rich learning journey is, when one considers the cost of recruitment or internal selection, minimal to the point of being irrelevant.

And yet most organizations do little to enrich the integration process. Search consultants the world over seem to ignore what in any other sphere would be considered normal "after sales service." Human Resource departments talk eloquently about the need to measure intellectual capital but do little of consequence to protect and, in a meaningful sense, leverage that investment.

The answer, in part, is that people are too busy. For many managers and executives, success has become a seven-day-a-week struggle. Ironically, it is exactly those competitive and driven individuals, the ones who dig deepest into their own resources, who are best positioned to make the greatest contribution to a new executive's integration.

There is perhaps another reason integration is inadequately supported and this one lies sadly at the very core of the organizations we have created: the modern enterprise is not a place where the notion of caring carries with it a great deal of cachet.

It hasn't always been this way. Before empowerment, before TQM, before globalization and even before the emergence of high-tech warrior leaders, many organizations contained within them a thread of community. Inefficient, exploitative, ponderous, paternalistic they may have been, but for many they represented and were spoken of as "our place."

Those who spend time with executives, regardless of where they come from in the world, find stark and undeniable evidence of a modern organizational malaise: ruthlessness and a slash-and-burn attitude are admired; older workers are cast aside in favor of younger and "cheaper" replacements; the size of an executive's pay check often bears little relationship to his/her actual contribution; and the exploitation of children in the third world is seen as an unfortunate but "necessary" business practice. Even that old standby, "loyalty" has lost its worth in today's survival stakes. There is a profound human and overwhelming business need to reinvent the modern organization. The stark reality: today's "head and hand" leadership destroys the human spirit as surely as did the assembly line in its day.

Is it any wonder that many young executives believe that taking a job is not about making a contribution but about what the role will do to make his or her resume look stronger? Commonplace are the talented information technology specialists under thirty-five who move to another organization at the drop of a hat. Executive search consultants are finding an ever more receptive ear even amongst those working for leading edge organizations. For many, nay the majority, the dollar, the franc, the pound, the lira have become the only real currency in job progression and career planning.

It is from within this potent brew that the new executive has to think about career. Those who move for personal gain will rise quickly but will soon find that their experience, because they rarely stay around long enough to see the product of their decision-making, will be their Achilles' heel as they move into more senior roles. Conversely, those who tie themselves to the mast of one ship will go down with it if it flounders. The key is balance: to stay in one role too long is clearly limiting; and to move too soon detracts from the quality and depth of the learning.

Balance is the common feature of those who seem to have the most favorable passage. Joining an organization that sees investment in people as a low priority makes sense only if the executive in question intends to use the role as a stepping stone to something else. Even then, in a world of rapid obsolescence, most such moves prove to be career traps from which the executive **can't** progress. On the other hand, those who hand total responsibility for their development over to the organization are no less foolish.

What follows are the building blocks of career that the promoted or incoming executive should take into account as he or she strikes that balance, as he or she navigates a future course.

Career planning starts with success in the current role

Arthur Hoppe once said: "We all worry about the population explosion, but we don't worry about it at the right time." The same is true of career planning; most people worry about where their career is headed but they worry about it too late. Career thinking should anticipate and build a strategy to respond to the possibility of corporate downsizing, merger, economic downturn, unique opportunity and the like. It should not be the outcome of a forced, defensive response. One group forced to take career planning seriously are those receiving outplacement support. When urgency speaks, what is important seems to have a way of emerging naturally.

Any meaningful journey has to have two points of calibration: a destination and a precise location of where one is now. Much of the literature and general hyperbole about taking charge of one's career focuses on the destination. But career planning starts and **must** start with success in the current role. In sales, it's an old adage that keeping current customers is a lot easier than finding new ones. In career planning, leveraging current success is a lot easier than starting afresh.

Chapter five outlines the importance of leadership (there is a world of difference between leadership and leading) and the critical questions to pose to get a handle on the new role. Chapter seven describes the importance of agreeing on an agenda and setting priorities. Both of these chapters cover materials that are essential building blocks in defining success in the new role. There is one more critical step: outlining the behavior (competency) that is necessary for success in the new role.

Leading edge organizations build their recruitment, succession and management development actions on well thought through competency profiles for **all** of the key roles. Enlightened organizations train their leaders to develop competency profiles as part of a meaningful focus on coaching. The probability is that you are on your own.

The fact that a competency outline has already been developed does not mean that the promoted or incoming executive must pin this by the mirror and repeat it every morning. Every executive will see the role a little differently. What was important yesterday may not be as critical today. Priorities change. But this will provide an excellent starting point for defining success.

Competency is not about describing adequate, good enough, survival-oriented performance. To be a true benchmark for performance success, a competency profile must capture the sum and substance of what **excellence** looks and feels like.

Competency is something like a tree or an iceberg — the most important bits, what makes them potent, the origin of their strength, lies below the surface. The lack of a well thought out competency profile is one reason many recruitment decisions turn out badly. Ships and organizations alike get sunk by what lies *beneath* the surface.

The term "behavior" is thrown around a lot by consultants and Human Resource practitioners. The literal definition of behavior is *"the way in which an organism works; the way something reacts to its environment."* Behavioral scientists have created a different meaning in which behavior is defined as *"outwardly observable behavior."* The term "competency" avoids confusion by describing both overt, observable behavior – head and the hand - **and** that which often lies below the surface – heart and spirit.

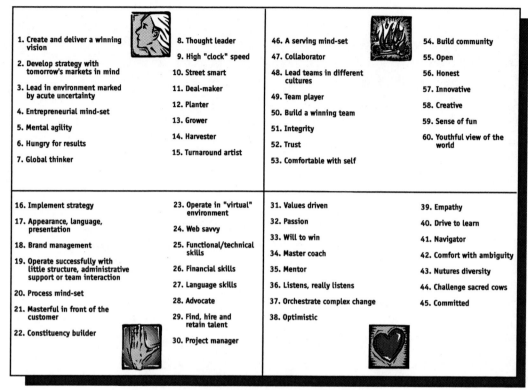

1. Create and deliver a winning vision	8. Thought leader	46. A serving mind-set	54. Build community
2. Develop strategy with tomorrow's markets in mind	9. High "clock" speed	47. Collaborator	55. Open
3. Lead in environment marked by acute uncertainty	10. Street smart	48. Lead teams in different cultures	56. Honest
4. Entrepreneurial mind-set	11. Deal-maker	49. Team player	57. Innovative
5. Mental agility	12. Planter	50. Build a winning team	58. Creative
6. Hungry for results	13. Grower	51. Integrity	59. Sense of fun
7. Global thinker	14. Harvester	52. Trust	60. Youthful view of the world
	15. Turnaround artist	53. Comfortable with self	

16. Implement strategy	23. Operate in "virtual" environment	31. Values driven	39. Empathy
17. Appearance, language, presentation	24. Web savvy	32. Passion	40. Drive to learn
18. Brand management	25. Functional/technical skills	33. Will to win	41. Navigator
19. Operate successfully with little structure, administrative support or team interaction	26. Financial skills	34. Master coach	42. Comfort with ambiguity
20. Process mind-set	27. Language skills	35. Mentor	43. Nutures diversity
21. Masterful in front of the customer	28. Advocate	36. Listens, really listens	44. Challenge sacred cows
22. Constituency builder	29. Find, hire and retain talent	37. Orchestrate complex change	45. Committed
	30. Project manager	38. Optimistic	

Leadership Competencies

Figure 23

Describing the critical competencies should not be a complex or overly elaborate exercise. The rule is to keep it simple. **Figure 23** outlines the competencies – drawn out of the author's work on leadership and skewed towards a Hunter-Gatherer business model (see chapter two) – that, when reflected upon, allows the new executive to build a competency profile for his/her role. The meta-question that acts as a frame for capturing the competencies is "What is it that differentiates an outstanding performer from one who is merely middle of the road?"

The value in exploring a generic list of competencies is that it stimulates thinking and poses challenging questions about focus. The new executive should see Figure 23, however, as merely initiating his/her thinking. A starting point, because a list of competencies, no matter how well thought through, cannot be stretched to meet every situation. A place to begin, because there is tremendous value in the new executive building on the language that has currency within the organization/culture.

In drawing together the critical competencies, five "canons" should be borne in mind:

1. If the role is poorly defined then it follows that any ensuing competency profile can be no more than a house built on sand.

2. Identifying more than 7-10 competencies mitigates against the need for focus. Some would suggest that 5 – 8 is a more suitable number.

3. The competencies identified must be thought of in terms of "absolute," "must have," "can't succeed without this attribute," characteristics of success.

4. The leadership competencies outlined are intended to complement (role specific), not override or be a substitute for any organization-wide, leadership competencies.

5. Although there may be skewing towards the heart and the spirit, a competency profile that ignores the head and the hand lacks balance.

The competency profile should be soberly reviewed and form the basis of a personal development plan. Mentor support, building a coaching relationship with the hiring executive, and even translating the competency profile into a 360° review are all valuable means whereby shortfalls can be addressed.

Building a competency profile should not rest with the role that the new executive has been handed. There is real value in building a competency profile focusing on how the new executive believes the role will unfold; building a profile of what success will look like one to two years out. Understanding today's competencies builds a platform for performance excellence. Understanding tomorrow's competencies sets the stage for future success. Both are critical.

Figure 24 outlines the competency profile for the President of a high-tech start up as first outlined (role profile) in chapter five.

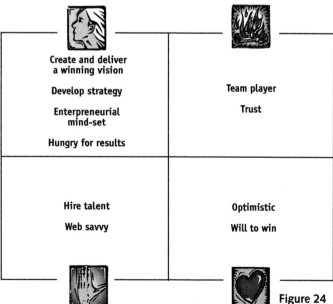

Create and deliver a winning vision

Develop strategy

Enterpreneurial mind-set

Hungry for results

Team player

Trust

Hire talent

Web savvy

Optimistic

Will to win

Figure 24

Competency Profile: President High-tech Start Up

Knowing how to swim isn't enough - those in the water have to be on the look out for the next big wave

It is never too early for a new executive to start developing, or in some cases refining, their career plan. To put it off because you think there is too much change to make a plan useful is like a sailor putting off charting a route because the winds are too strong. Oh you'll end up somewhere all right, but it'll be mighty crowded and you'll be damn lucky if there's anything to see there. Napoleon understood better than anyone that strategy ended once the first cannon was fired. But his preparation, focus on training, and ability to pick the ground were, nevertheless, the basis of many a dramatic victory.

By the same token no meaningful personal work around career can afford to ignore tomorrow's uncertainty. Central to any career thinking has to be a sense of reality: a focus on personal flexibility; and a discipline around learning how to learn. Preparing for tomorrow's uncertainty also means considering the changing societal context within which issues such as personal growth and quality of life are likely to unfold.

Outlining likely future trends is, of course, incomplete unless it includes a wee bit of skepticism. There are flash in the pan trends and then there are those that have staying power. A number of ongoing trends are writ so large that it would be foolish to ignore them.

- *Traditional notions of career are redundant.* Anyone under forty who thinks they will end their career doing the same sort of work that they currently do does not have their eyes open. Similarly, any one under thirty whose plan of action assumes two, three or even four separate careers before they hang up their boots is on the right track. When even that stalwart of presumed job security, the auditor, is under attack, no one should presume they will stay the course. Merger, smarter clients, the use of information technology, the nimbleness of boutique competitors, and consolidation of global audit firms (read down-sizing) have meant that the working world has become a realm where new ideas and a comfort with uncertainty are the order of the day.

- *There is a new definition of literacy.* We live in a society where technology equals infor-mation overload. A hundred television channels are shortly to become five hundred. A thousand lies on the horizon. Information, however, is not the same as knowledge. The latter means not only being able to organize data but being able to make sense of it.

- *The Internet is all pervasive.* A single global telephone number will mean that any one of us can be accessed by any one of the other six billion people on the earth instantly, 24 hours a day. Access, however, is not the same as being available. Listening to and watching world events condensed into thirty-second "news bites" is not to be confused with being informed.   Being opinionated is not the same as having an opinion. Marshall McLuhan and Bruce Powers wrote: "Western man now discovers himself habitually relating to information structures which are simultaneous, discontinuous, and dynamic. He has been plunged into a form of knowing, far from his customary experience tied to the printed page" (*The Global Village*, pg. 14).

Being literate is not the same as literacy. Full literacy in today's context is a new form of knowing that is both right and left-brain. It is a knowing that recognizes and transcends cultural boundaries. It is a way of knowing that encompasses the skills necessary to travel the communication highways, a way of knowing that is built on the ability to not only access but to define what is truly important. A way of knowing that embraces how to share knowledge and with whom. A way of knowing that turns imagery, symbolism, story, and learning through play into a way to be. It is a way of knowing that is integral to success in the new Millennium. It is a way of knowing that is central to career growth, self-leadership and, as a result, intrapersonal harmony.

- *Few of us should plan to retire.*   The probability of having the kind of retirement envisioned by our fathers and mothers is slim. Demographics, structured unemployment, budget deficits, downloading of central government costs, an attention to health and fitness, diet, late families, and expanding economies in the third world all combine to make retirement at sixty, sixty-five, or even seventy years of age a vague hope for Mr. and Mrs. Everybody. The totally self-interested baby boomers have located the font of wisdom in their generation for, well, a generation, so no one should be surprised when all of a sudden, as they age, the status of the elder person is valued. They will represent a powerful social and economic gray force, and when positioned in a business environment that values experience-based forms of knowledge (e.g., Organization change, Mergers and Acquisitions, Legal advice, Therapy), they will be highly sought after. This means that for many executives - if they equip themselves to do so - an active career that continues well into later life, is not only possible, but financially desirable.

For many it will mean retraining. For all, it will mean working differently: learning how to consult, polishing writing skills, making presentation a core competency, being comfortable as an advisor/mentor. There is a major win-win-win here. First, society will not be prone to cast aside intellectual capital based on some arbitrary notion such as age. Second, an engaged, energetic, informed, non-competitive, mature set of advisors/consultants/ part-time executives, cast forth within the overall business world can be a major force for community building. Last but not least, their access to financial resources, and their sense of work as an ongoing source of energy and self-esteem, will enrich many an older couple's lives who, in the past, might have expected no better than to slink off to Sun City to join the newly wed and the nearly dead. Not that there's anything wrong with that.

- *The world really is getting smaller.* Leading edge consultants who used to only get calls from domestic clients now find that their work takes them literally anywhere in the world. To lose an order to an established competitor has never been an easy thing to accept. It is even more difficult to rationalize when that order is lost to an unknown competitor from a country that is hard to find on the map, something more sales executives are experiencing these days. Notwithstanding the ease at which, for a price, talent can be plucked out of even leading edge firms, the quality of leadership demanded for many opportunities means that a purely domestic search is impractical.

  Today's purchasing agent is a citizen of the world. Software is as likely to come from a vendor in India, or Sheffield, England, as it is from one of the established high-tech corridors. Career thinking by a leader that doesn't see the world as essentially without borders, that doesn't assume a work-life that encompasses several countries, that doesn't take account of a need for languages and a global mind-set, is fundamentally flawed.

- *The collapse of hierarchy has changed irrevocably how career progression is measured.* It was not that long ago that career progression was marked by a series of ever upward steps, each marked by a new title that carried with it an instant designation as to where the individual stood in the organizational hierarchy. A Senior Vice President clearly outranked a mere Vice President who in turn outranked an Assistant Vice President and so forth. Full house over two pair. Indeed, attempting to deconstruct what in many organizations is still the established order of things is, even today, akin to putting one's hand in the lion's cage. But for the most part, the toppling of the organizational pyramid means that career progression based exclusively on hierarchical level has little meaning. Taking its place are measures of career growth based on potential contribution, the nature of the strategic landscape, the importance of the role to the organization overall, the complexity being faced, the maturity of the team, and the inherent challenge involved in delivering value for the customer.

- *Don't buck demographics.* Amongst the wealth of research that is available to support career planning, demographic data should be considered prime. Or as David Foote, the Canadian demographer, likes to say, demographics explain about two thirds of everything (*Boom, Bust and Echo* pg. 2). The age makeup of the population significantly impacts trends and buying patterns in areas as diverse as fashion, real estate, sports, travel, tourism, music, computer sales, mini vans, public transport, the stock market, the sale of beer - and virtually anything else one might like to think of.

There is no substitute for having been there

The world of sports can be overrated as a model for business. Coaching a one-in-a-million, two-million dollars in endorsements type athlete is hardly the same thing as trying to inspire a 60-year old supervisor in a run down, cash short, heavily unionized, rust-belt factory, who, regardless of the company's results, will still get his or her full pension in five years' time. But at the same time, when thinking about the top end performers, there are similarities.

To make it to the major leagues, a young baseball player will have had to ride an endless series of buses to nowhere USA; he will have had to hone his skills in ballparks that he himself had to maintain; and he will have been tried out in virtually every field position to find where his talents lie. No one on Manchester United's first team made it to stardom without spending a great deal of time in the minor and junior leagues. Athletics, cricket, basketball, cycle racing, the story is the same. What's more, none of today's established stars progressed simply because of age, the sort of school he or she went to, or personal connections. Regardless of the sport, athletes move to the top of their profession based on one simple criterion – his or her ability to figuratively, and sometimes literally, **put the puck in the net**.

The best experience for running a big business is to run a small one, **successfully**. The best training to become a department head is to have headed up a smaller team **successfully**.

The best test of fit for a business turnaround challenge is to have **successfully** turned around other businesses. Being a number 2 in a large enterprise is useful, even invaluable. Being at the shoulder of the master often entails a series of powerful learning events, but it is still no substitute for the experience gained by being an actual leader.

Career planning is about creating choices. It is also about understanding what it takes to succeed, and being prepared **to spend time in the trenches** learning both the art and the craft of leadership. Management education is invaluable - to say it is essential would be an overstatement since many make it to the top without that "advantage" - but no one should be fooled into thinking that an MBA or any other set of advanced academic qualifications are substitutes for having been there. The key, as always, is balance, balance, and balance.

The prudent executive thinks of him or herself as a one-person business

Chapter four outlines the thinking a promoted or incoming executive would be advised to go through to better understand the context within which his or her new role is set. Attempting to come to terms with what drives the business is work that executives are both comfortable with, and good at. If asked, few executives would decry the need and benefit of a well thought through strategy.

It is astonishing therefore that, when asked, those same executives, those same driven individuals whose temperament invariably means that they absolutely revel in solving the subtle challenges and puzzles that impede competitiveness, have no idea whatsoever about how to apply those same skills and qualities to their own career.

Thinking of yourself as a one-person business is a potent way to think through career issues. The questions that follow from this thinking are the meat and potatoes of any successful career strategy.

- What is my mission? Why am I doing this? When I'm retired and I look back, what do I want to be proud of? If I could leave a heritage, what would it be? If I'm successful, who benefits? Who loses out?

- Could I without hesitation and in clear, crisp language, outline exactly the role and the sort of work I want to be doing ten years from now? Moreover, could I describe specifically why the role I have today is helping me achieve that personal vision?

- What are my values? Is the work I am currently engaged in congruent with my values? Is there a fit between the organization's values and my personal values? If not, where is the misalignment? What needs to change?

- Is a there richness in my work that allows me to grow as both a manager and as a human being? If not, wherein lies the joy? If this is not nurturing my inner-self, why am I doing it?

- What are my own core competencies? What am I uniquely good at? Does my current role build on those strengths? Can the role be reframed such that my strengths can be brought out? Are there any other roles within the corporation that are a better fit with my competencies? If the answer is yes, what role(s) in particular would be better aligned with where I want to be ten years from now?

- If the organization were to be taken over by a competitor and I was made redundant next week, what would I do on the following Monday? Could I support my family as an independent consultant for a period of time? Recognizing that transition and change are natural elements of today's turbulent times, what do I need to do to give myself and my family personal security?

- Do I think of my skills and competencies as a business would think of its product or service? Do I market myself effectively both within and external to the firm? Have I thought of myself as a brand? What have I done to create brand recognition: written articles? given presentations? been on external professional bodies that have high visibility?

- Do I have an up-to-date resume that outlines my current contribution? Do I test the market at least once a year to get a better understanding of my currency in the job market?

- What issues lie on the horizon? How will the job market unfold? What social, political and economic issues do I need to take into account? Does the direction I am charting recognize and take advantage of these forces?

- From a leadership perspective, is my ability being fully used? What is the price to be paid by taking the next step? Am I willing to pay that price?

- In my current role, whom do I serve? Am I enriched by that experience? What could I do differently to make the experience more meaningful? Who should I be serving beyond those mentioned?

- Am I successful? How do I measure success? Is that measure meaningful? To what extent is quality of life factored into those criteria?

- Do I have a personal learning plan to be everything that I have the capacity to be within my new role? Do I have a personal development plan that will help me move into the role beyond this one? Are these reviewed regularly? Is energy and time going into their accomplishment? If not, what needs to happen?

- Do I have someone I respect to sit down with to challenge my career thinking? Have I, in the past, had conversations of this kind regularly? If not, what actions can be set in place to make this a reality in my new role?

Career planning is a matter of where you are and when

Career thinking for an executive in the later years should clearly be based on different assumptions than those informing the direction taken by someone just starting out. Arguably there are five distinct career stages, as follows:

- *Stage 1, learning the ropes.* Early career experience has a profound effect on long-term career success. It is in these early formative years that a young man or woman builds an understanding of the overall business landscape. Their overall business philosophy, and their standards for key issues such as performance, business ethics, integrity, management style, respect for others, self-awareness, and serving the customer, all flow from the role modeling, values, disciplines and learning habits of early business experience.

  It is no accident that "graduates" from organizations such as General Electric, Shell, and Procter and Gamble are highly sought after in their thirties. Lateral, broad-based, experience with one outstanding organization is often far more marketable than job-hopping.

- *Stage 2, finding one's feet.* It is important that those with the drive, capability and desire to move into top leadership roles get "hands on" experience relatively early on. This is the time for a young man or woman to explore his or her own potential, to expand managerial skills and to develop the tools of the trade. International exposure is especially meaningful. It is essential that a younger executive at this stage of his or her career stay around long enough to have to deal with, or indeed take pleasure from, the fruits of their decision-making.

- *Stage 3, building success.* This is the time when a young executive must build a track record, must put some runs on the scoreboard. Success at this stage will open doors and opportunity for more significant roles later on. The scope and nature of the challenge faced will determine the size of the "credit" being created. Assuming general management is on the agenda, this is the time for a functional specialist to move into what has traditionally been called a line role.

- *Stage 4, making experience count.* Despite exceptional stories to the contrary, these are the golden years of contribution for an executive. This is when he or she puts it all together, when he or she has the maturity to know and the self-confidence to act on what is possible.

- *Stage 5, passing the baton.* At this final stage of career, family issues and lifestyle come to the fore. Lifestyle and balance become important here, as does a sense of wanting to leave a legacy. In the future it is likely that this stage will extend well beyond what has been the historical retirement age. Indeed, there is already evidence of an emerging sixth stage of career.

Each career stage is a period where the learning involved is an invaluable building block for later success. Is there an ideal time to move into a new role? If there is one, it is when one career stage is coming to an end and new horizons beckon.

Be prepared to stand naked

All of us, at one point or another in our careers, are confronted with "moments of truth," critical times when we have to make the decision to jump or stay put.

Sometimes it is the realization that a course taken, or an expectation assumed, was based on a false premise. The most difficult moments are those when failure, poor decision-making, lack of a critical skill, or missed targets have to be confronted. At such times, we can soften the harshness of the light shining on our limitations by rationalization, subtle self-deception and inner dialogue that puts the blame on others.

A more courageous and uplifting approach is to see such moments of behavioral nakedness as rare opportunities to examine the real self. Role shift is emotionally draining exactly because our inadequacies, lack of knowledge and inexperience, become painfully apparent. The executive who gets defensive, builds protective routines to mask his or her emotional vulnerability, is stripping the integration experience of those moments of self-awareness that are the very foundation of wisdom, mastery and maturity.

Passion is the source of true excellence

Life is short and, in the developed world, quite a bit of it is going to be spent on that series of linked activities we call "work." But that is what society expects of us. The Anglo Saxon work ethic has impacted belief systems well beyond the boundaries of its European origins. It wasn't by accident that the ultimate statement of rebellion of the sixties was "to drop out."

When asked why they work, people at all levels invariably give very mundane reasons: "We need to work to live." "I have to work to support my children." "Work is the means through which I can create the financial resources to do other things." "I would love to retire but I have to work." "It is true that there are other things that I could do but I wouldn't earn as much money!" Money figures highly because it seems satisfaction is presumed to be a forbidden fruit.

These are not the answers of the artist, the musician or even the dedicated scientist. They talk about their work from an entirely different perspective. For the artist, and those of their kind, work gives life meaning. Work serves the artist's passion, nurtures his or her spirit, and provides a sense of joy. For the artist, work is a truly enriching activity. For some, it is even a spiritual experience. The artist describes a special sort of experience, one that Mihaly Csikszentmihalyi calls being in FLOW.

But then why should just the newly appointed executive lay out a schema for personal growth? Why would any of us settle for anything less? Settling means turning our backs on the source of true excellence.

Joseph Campbell perhaps captured best the power of tapping into our inner resources when he said, "if you do follow your bliss you put yourself on a kind of track that has been there all the while, waiting for you, and the life that you ought to be living is the one you are living. When you see that, you begin to meet people who are in the field of your bliss, and they open the doors to you. I say, follow your bliss and don't be afraid, and doors will open where you didn't know they were going to be" (*The Power of Myth*, pg. 120).

Integration into a new role is more than a survival skill, it is at heart about putting in place the building blocks of future success. Day-to-day work pressures, doing more with less, picking the kids up from day care, all distract us from spending quality time thinking about "Where is this headed?" "What does it mean?" "How do I get a degree of control?"

Career planning has to go beyond being a mechanical exercise in deciding what the next job should be. To be meaningful it has to answer the wider questions of self-identity, quality of life, community service, passion, and spiritual enrichment. None of us should, or can, lead compartmentalized lives.

Thinking about our career is thinking about our life and the value we bring to others. Putting career thinking on hold is putting our lives on hold. It is not an important part of moving into a new role, it is the culmination of the thinking that runs through the other eight chapters; it is the outcome of successfully transforming what, for many, is a burden into a rich and unforgettable learning experience.

Chapter Nine

Critical Learning

- It is never too early for the new executive to start developing or redefining his/her career plan.

- Career planning starts with success in the current role.

- Career planning is about creating choices and understanding what it takes to succeed.

- The prudent executive thinks of him/herself as a one person business.

- Career planning is largely a matter of where you are – when.

- Each of us must be prepared to "stand naked."

- Passion is the true source of excellence.

Consequences

If you don't manage your career, someone else will!

Step back and reflect on the ideas that surfaced and the learning you take from this chapter. Consider the path you are on, the need to build relationships (fit), and your understanding of success in the new role (expectations). Think about what you need to stop doing, start doing, and that which you need to do differently.

_____

_____

_____

_____

_____

_____

_____

_____

_____

_____

_____

Completing the weave

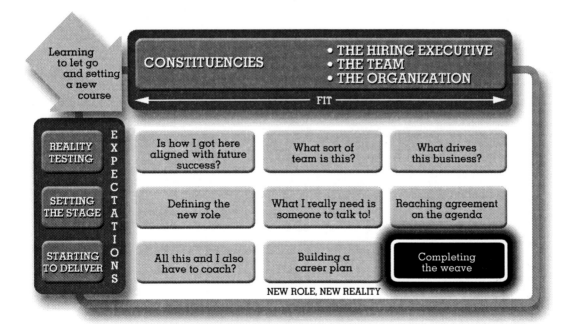

Completing the weave

In thinking about your new role you will have gone through each chapter carefully. Each is a critical building block in the integration process.

This final chapter is somewhat different. It does not contain a set of things to do. It does not pose new questions. There are no conceptual diagrams to ponder. It is more philosophical than directive. And although it is strong in imagery and metaphor it does not break new ground. There are, however, two reasons why this chapter is important. The first: it summarizes and consolidates much that has been introduced elsewhere in the book. As such it enriches the reader's overall learning. It is a vehicle for reflection. And, make no mistake, reflection is essential if lasting learning is to emerge. The second: the book is built around the belief that those privileged enough to lead, if they are to succeed, must strike a balance between the head, the hand, the heart, and the spirit. This chapter deepens and enriches what is meant by the two elements that are missing from the current leadership agenda – engaging the heart and enriching the spirit. This chapter completes the weave.

If there is a third reason for the material contained within this chapter, it is to bridge the learning of the integration process with the period beyond integration: consolidation and growth. We would ask you to read the chapter with one important question in mind. As I move forward what do I need to do to be the difference that makes a difference?

Angels with only one wing each of us may be, but when we have the courage to reach out and embrace each other we are destined to soar.

* * * * *

Winter is rightly a time of discontent. Spring, with all its promise, emerges violently from its hidden caverns. Summer produces not growth but stilted examples of what might have been. Autumn, the season of color, of abundance, of bounty, of harvest in all of its glory, is scarce present. A cold wind is blowing through the land!

The allegory is of the seasons, but the cold breath of nature speaks of leadership. It describes unfulfilled promise. Unfulfilled because, despite the intense focus over the past two decades, leadership still represents the chief malady of organizational performance. The evidence: 80% plus of major change initiatives fail, the vast majority of mergers and acquisitions do not deliver on that promised, there is little correlation between IT spending and business results, the recruitment lag for the right person to steer a troubled organization through heavy seas is 12 months or more. If the role is global, shout for your chequebook. McKinsey, the consulting firm, even talks of the "War for Talent." Loss of loyalty, burnout, an inability to deal with the emerging complexity, cultural myopia, a win-lose mentality, short-term predatory buying practices – they all blow the weathervane in the direction of a leadership malaise.

There are, of course, success stories. Our leaders have been well trained in the science, although less well in the art, of strategy. By the multitude they can measure, analyze, refine, budget, and work the numbers such that financial engineering has come to contain within it an elegant beauty all of its own. The market place has been segmented, and segmented, and will, no doubt, be segmented many times more. Today's channels of distribution would be alien to someone who retired even as little as 12 or 18 months ago. Those who preach of core business competencies have raised their intellectual wards to the status of superstars. Winter is all that could be asked of it. Leadership as defined by the head is alive and thriving – as, indeed, it must be.

The story doesn't end there. The power of technology, end-to-end value chains, the process organization, the ability to run international projects around the world 24 hours a day, improved cycle times, managing knowledge, brand management, flattened structures, minimal bureaucracy, six sigma, JIT, infrastructure management, benchmarking, smart systems, reengineering, aggressive outsourcing – they all speak of value creation. Spring is in full bloom. Leadership, as represented by the hand, is a gardener's delight – as indeed, it must be.

But what of the insufficiency? There is a yearning in the land - a cry for something beyond that being offered. It is more than a cry, it is a chorus, one that has reached a crescendo where the common voice is: **What about me!** Each year we train thousands of businessmen and women. What has somehow been lost is that leadership isn't just about measures and processes and/or things; leadership, when all is said and done, is a noble calling – it is about enriching people's lives. Leadership is a privilege. It is a sacred trust.

Nature's plan lies not within any single season but in its unfolding unity. Each season is a special time, but it is the whole that yields nature's wealth. So it is with leadership. Leadership that defines the *mission* is of the head (winter). Leadership that generates *movement* is of the hand (spring). Leadership that builds through *mastery* must touch people's hearts (summer). Leadership that provides *meaning* has to encompass the spirit (autumn). **Only when all of the seasons are "full," only when each unfolds one unto another can leadership bring about a transformation.** Only when the *leadership weave* is complete can leadership be the difference that makes a difference. The reality: creating a loyal and vital community counts for naught if the competition is eating your lunch. Conversely, in that it continuously diminishes the only sustainable means to differentiate and compete, leadership that originates only from the head and hand destroys value – it strips the organization of emotional capital. For people to give *of themselves* they need to feel that to change is to step into the light. For people to be deeply committed, they have to believe that the journey they are being asked to take is one that has personal meaning. What people are yearning for are leaders who can not only address the head and deliver the hand, *but also engage the heart and enrich the spirit*. There is overwhelming evidence to support the contention that many of us are well versed in the head and hand. None of us can become masterful leaders, however, until we *complete the weave*.

Engaging the heart

The head frames *direction*. The hand describes *the how*. The heart is engaged when people know, **really know**, *why!* Work that demands stretch, responsibility that empowers, customers who are delighted, openness of communication, dialogue, understanding, ownership, and involvement, all transform apathy into appetite; turn a willingness to go along into a desire to excel. Learning and growth enrich the heart. To appeal to the heart is to incite passion and commitment.

Organizations spawned over the past two hundred years have been the product of two far-reaching assumptions. The first: without extensive rules, policies and procedures, people will act irresponsibly. The second: the best way to organize an enterprise is to create simple jobs linked together by complex processes. The first destroys trust. The second robs those involved of any feelings of personal worth. To touch people's hearts is to reach into every far corner and purge the enterprise of these beliefs. Leaders who engage the heart build from the premise of trust.

Language and imagery touch the heart. A lame, "me too," one-dimensional picture of tomorrow is a mandate for mediocrity. A vision that fails to present a vivid, vibrant, compelling future is a signal that the organization is destined to be forever becalmed. Metaphors and symbols that exalt the kill, but omit the warrior's reverence for the prey, define a "hunt" devoid of honor. Language that excludes, that limits, that restricts, that belittles, that signals elitism, that is about ego, that dwells unnecessarily on yesterday, that reinforces hierarchical power, that is about the act of bosship, that puts down the customer, that seeks to control, creates a toxic environment that breeds cynicism and, at the first sign of difficulty, despair. Language that sings of the possible, that challenges, that celebrates, that shares, that affirms, that encourages, that is woven into positive story, that sparkles with humor, that is rooted in modesty, that is filled with wisdom, is language that engages the heart. Leaders understand that language isn't merely important, they act with the knowledge that language is everything.

The change of cadence and rhythm that accompanies new patterns of play engages the heart. Champions are nourished not by what worked yesterday but by the opportunity to move into new space. The presumption that new behaviors cannot emerge from entrenched ways is to admit defeat before the clash of battle is enjoined. Championships are won by the unexpected, by the bold act the opposition had not planned for, by a finely honed sense of the "moment." The best strategy is to ask what is the most damaging thing the competition can do, and do it first. New patterns create new opportunity. Leaders who make a difference constantly change their own patterns of play.

There are four ways to "know." There is the knowing of the head, the knowing that comes from analysis, study and presentation. There is the knowing of the hand that comes from a sense of kinetic awareness, from touching, through observation. There is knowing from the heart, an intuitive sense of what feels right. And there is the knowing rooted in the spirit, a deep inner awareness that connects self, time, and purpose. Knowing from the head and the hand translates data into information. Knowing from the heart and spirit transforms information into knowledge and, when complemented by rich experience, into a quality best described as wisdom. Leaders who make critical decisions based on *knowing* that is skewed heavily to the head and hand are ignoring the reality that much of what they are measuring and even observing is either out of date, or redundant. In a world where speed of response, organizational agility, and an ability to manage uncertainty rule, leaders destined to thrive are those who, when the situation demands it, listen to their heart and trust their spirit.

Values touch people's hearts. Here we speak not of organizational values - invariably generated with the naive assumption that organizations can create, without factoring in people's emerging wants, aspirations and desires, something called *a culture* - but of the concerns and needs of those who make the organization work. Organizational values may touch people's hearts, often they don't. Few front-line employees get up with the lark, have a sparkle in their eye, and a spring in the step, and a song on their lips, all inspired by the thought of getting to work early to *create shareholder value*. Organizational values are of the head. People's personal values are of the heart. Leaders who make a difference build alignment between organizational and personal values.

An interesting question is to ask someone who has achieved success, "Who or what was it that made the difference in your life?" The answer invariably points to someone who listened, someone who inspired, someone who took the time, someone who gave them the strength to follow their passion, someone who encouraged them to soar - a teacher, a mentor, a coach. To share of one's self is to engage the heart. To share one's story and to guide a colleague, peer, or subordinate through and past the waiting organizational pitfalls, is to engage the heart. To provide the context, the challenge, the opportunity, and to give honest feedback, with the result that a subordinate and/or team member embraces his/her full potential, is to engage the heart. Leaders who make a difference **always** make the time to teach, mentor, and coach.

There is no magic, no secret elixir, and no hidden formula to hiring and keeping talent. People are drawn to organizations where they feel they can grow and make a difference. People decide to stay when they feel that they are being listened to, are informed as to what is going on, know themselves to be successful and believe that regardless of what happens to the business they have currency in the job market. If there is a common thread that links these attributes, it is learning. Leaders who make a difference are those who build awareness through rich conversation. Leaders who sustain are those who have a passion to learn.

Learning is of the heart. New ways to be necessitates new ways to learn. Invaluable as training and instruction are, they are not the means whereby people see their work anew. A world being continuously transformed means that those who stand in the eye of the storm must be capable of navigating even when the wind, rain and lightning crash together with full force. For the leader, it means that traditional forms of learning must give way to *learning how to learn*. This, in turn, means that the learning must be elegantly crafted to fit the context. Three routes, in particular, lie open. The first, learning based on and drawn out of the experience of others: case study, business simulation, implementing best practice developed elsewhere. The second, where the learner moves to the center of the arena and where the boundaries have a degree of stretch, e.g. the freedom to act that underscores true employee empowerment. The third, where the learner defines not only the learning process but what is possible e.g. the freedom that research engineers are given at 3M. Leadership that engages the heart recognizes and acts on the belief that *how* people learn is more important than *what* they learn.

Recent times have seen a renaissance in what is often described as "experiential learning." A wilderness experience, ropes programs, drumming, river rafting, building a children's playground in a poor part of the city, all represent examples of *learning by doing*. Consistent with Howard Gardner's theories on multiple intelligence, the essence of experience-based learning is that learning cannot be compartmentalized - it must be made whole. If the emotional dimension of learning is ignored then much of what it takes to succeed is ignored. If people don't have an opportunity to "touch" their personal edge they are likely to remain ignorant of what they are truly capable of. Teamwork cannot be taught, it can only be lived. Spirit remains a vague and ephemeral concept until the team finds itself lost in the Canadian wilderness. Leaders who make a difference understand that successful learning is a holistic, full-bodied experience that appeals to the head, involves the hand, engages the heart, and enriches the spirit.

Empowerment is a term that carries with it a discordant echo. A litany of negligent implementation, lack of leadership, poor timing, and attempts to retrofit team-based processes into organization structures that emphasize hierarchy and the dominance of the individual have all brought empowerment initiatives into disrepute. The logic (head) of driving out cost that doesn't create customer value has all too often led to the last vestiges of employee loyalty (the heart) being ploughed under. Empowerment creates value when the head, the hand, the heart and the spirit are in balance. Empowerment initiatives have force when the following **ten** conditions have been met: (1) the organization's strategic intent is described by a robust, clear, and winning value proposition; (2) the organization structure and the way the organization moves information is defined by the organization's core business processes; (3) leadership shortfalls have been tackled; (4) the organization hierarchy is subordinate to process/value flow and unnecessary decision-making levels have been torn out; (5) those in functional roles measure their performance by the extent to which they have impacted customer (a real customer, one who signs a cheque) value; (6) those who work within the core processes have the freedom, responsibility, accountability and competency needed to make innovation and a sense of entrepreneurship central to their work; (7) the scope of an individual's work is defined not by the restrictive boundaries of a "job" but by the extent to which he/she can shape the nature of his/her contribution (role); (8) the work being undertaken matches opportunity with capability; (9) the choir and not the lone performer sets the rhythm of organization life; (10) the success of any empowerment initiatives are measured from the customer's perspective. Leadership that enriches the heart enacts empowerment not as yet one more way to reduce cost but as a means whereby people control their own destiny.

Leaders who touch people's hearts manage *through* exception not *by* exception. This means catching people doing it right and not sitting back until failure sets the tone for the relationship. It means celebrating success. It means voicing new ways to approach old problems and stimulating the flow of ideas and suggestions. It means mastery in listening. It means that those in key roles have to understand that the answers voiced are an outcome of the quality of the questions asked. It means that challenging mental models is more important than the assumption that there is a "right" strategy. It means that it is okay for the leader to say, "I don't know." Leaders who make a difference build on success. Leaders who challenge the status quo must be prepared to hear themselves ask "dumb" questions and act in unexpected ways. Leaders who touch people's hearts must be willing to, on occasion, embarrass themselves.

Dialogue is from the heart. Dialogue is a quality conversation where judgement is put on hold; assumptions of outcome, power, and status are parked; and where probing inquiry and time set aside for reflection are deemed a necessary prerequisite for new levels of understanding to emerge. Dialogue is the container whereby people buy-in to the *why*.

Dialogue and discussion are not the same. One is the art of the conductor who knows how and when to bring in different instruments such that the outcome is a rich sense of harmony. The other is the skill, knowledge and judgement of the tennis player where the laws of physics dictate that the ball will eventually come to rest on one side of the net. One relies on timing, empathy, and respect (heart); the other on an ability to solve problems (the head). Both are essential. Leaders who make a difference act only after seeing an important opportunity and/or critical problem through the eyes of the other stakeholders.

The heart is represented by summer. Summer is a time of learning. It is a time when questions posed during the winter and amplified during the spring, are answered. It is a time when nature moves to bring the reflection of winter and planting of the spring into fruition. It is a time of flow and light. Summer is when the leader champions, nurtures, and takes pride in growth.

Enriching the spirit

Spirit touches the deepest part of who we are. When we talk of spirit we are giving voice to that which is the very essence of one's way of life. Spirit is more than a description of behavior; more than a personal orientation; more than a song of the possible; spirit is, at its core, *a way to be*.

Spirit is sparked by actions that encompass value beyond personal gain. For the individual, it equates to success of the team. For the team, it means that the organization gains. For the organization, any meaningful definition of success must include the wider community. Leaders that compete successfully for people's commitment build their work around a mission that embodies within it a deep sense of purpose and meaning.

For the leader, spirit is anchored in a passionate desire to serve. Here we face a dilemma. For those brought up with English as a first language, "to serve" conjures up the sounds and pictures of *servitude*. Indeed, the British class system relegates those who serve to one of the lower rungs on the ladder of social importance. In the US "the leader as the lone hero" equates success with power, domination, and tough-mindedness. The language and imagery in other cultures is less restricting. In Finland, for example, to serve is captured by the word "hinku." Hinku speaks of not just the value of serving, but the enriching nature, dignity and personal growth that the act of serving embodies. Sustainable leadership, leadership that enriches the spirit, leadership that builds loyalty, leadership that transforms, can only emanate out of a personal feeling of hinku.

To listen to one's spirit is to know that loneliness and solitude are not the same thing. The former describes a separation, an unnatural state where an individual is like a flower or plant without water - starved of something vital to its growth and ultimate survival. Solitude, on the other hand, is time set aside to reflect and to deepen our understanding of where we are on our life's mission. Solitude is a natural, empowering and, arguably, essential dimension of knowing who we are. Solitude is a present we give ourselves when the forces that impact our lives are misaligned. Leaders who make a difference are deeply committed to the journey embarked on and are acutely conscious of a need to know and like themselves.

Few have had the joy of being a part of a truly great team. A great team transcends the ordinary, rejects mediocrity and eschews success based on past performance. A great team recognizes the individual while building a culture based on success of the whole. A great team relishes the sounds and feelings evoked by being at the edge. A great team has no weak members, only those who sing in a different key. A great team sees the impossible as merely another challenge and the extraordinary as a base camp for the next push up the mountain. When things go wrong, great teams change gears and put their foot to the floor. Great teams come to win and not to avoid defeat. Great teams don't have *failure* or *hoped for success* in their CD collection. Great teams live for the sound of winning. Great teams win. Great leaders build great teams.

The glue that bonds and connects those in a great team is spirit. It is a spirit nurtured not by a leader but by leadership. It is a spirit drawn out of a challenge that would sound discordant to an ordinary team. It is a spirit fueled by mutual respect, trust, and disdain for the status quo. It is a spirit that hugs opportunity and relishes risk. It is a spirit that revels in the duality of both belonging, and reaching out to include others. It is a spirit that surfaces in the sharing of best practice and a joy born out of the success of those who overcome adversity. It is a spirit apparent not only in the way success is celebrated but also in the generosity extended to those who stand on the podium in second place. Leaders who draw others to them display this generosity of spirit.

Spirit and truth cannot be separated. Here we speak not of the self-centered, manipulative mask of the egotist, but of the empathetic honesty that is the mark of maturity and comfort with self. It is a truth that lies not in the head but in the body. It is truth that underscores character, that shares success with others and admits failure early enough for counter measures to be put in place. It is truth that distinguishes criticism from meaningful and honest feedback. It is a truth that carries with it the echo of "I care." It is the truth of the coach who admits, "I am part of the problem here." It is the truth of the leader who listens to the audience, who knows what the players are capable of, where the edge of the stage is, and how to act when members of the cast fail to deliver the performance demanded.

Love and caring are of the heart. Courage draws on the spirit. It is the courage to act with boldness when others hold back. It is the courage to say no when political expediency makes "yes" the comfortable course of action. It is the courage to stand apart from the accepted way to be. It is the courage to rise when adversity, self-doubt and uncertainty cause one to stumble. It is the courage to challenge leadership that is not true to the values being espoused. It is the courage to step out of the way and allow others more qualified to make the decision. It is the courage to listen when the answer seems obvious. It is the courage to let go of behavior that no longer fits the current reality. It is the courage to know that unless I change, nothing changes. It is the courage needed to look into one's own heart. It is the courage to think deeply about issues that others face only in times of crisis: Does the work I am doing have meaning? Who gains? Am I personally growing? Is the way I learn aligned with the organization's culture? Are my personal values being fulfilled? Am I shortchanging those I love? Does what I'm doing engage my heart and enrich my spirit? Is my success based on what I take, or what I give? For the leader, courage is the capacity to bring about personal change, even move on, if the answer(s) that flow back do not resonate - if they do not strike a positive chord.

Spirit speaks of beliefs. For some, these beliefs are drawn from a religious doctrine or credo. For others, their beliefs are more secular in nature. Beliefs are the bedrock that anchors our view of the world. Meaning, inspiration and success are defined by our beliefs. One need look no further than shared beliefs to understand why many not-for-profit organizations draw thousands to their banner, people who are dedicated, work long hours and often do so for little or no remuneration.

Society is enabled and kept whole by its shared beliefs. Leaders who understand this also know that society at large ultimately plays a key role in setting the stage for spirit to emerge. Few, if any, employees ride to work to produce products that they have little pride in. If the question is health and safety there can only be one answer. No one in a modern society wants to add to the destruction of the planet. It is difficult to argue against honesty. Fairness is a doctrine that has been part of life's unfolding pattern since before the word took written form. Locking young people out of the job market invariably has long-term consequences. Outsourcing work to offshore locations that use production methods based on exploitation and unsafe practices condones and encourages such practices. Repetitive, soul-destroying work strips those so engaged of dignity and self-respect. It is difficult to suggest that tossing people aside like forgotten parts of a broken machine does anything other than unravel the weave of a caring society. Discrimination in its many forms destroys dreams. Only those who benefit directly support executive excess in the form of extravagant life styles. Leadership that enriches the spirit does so by recognizing, respecting, and *living up* to the beliefs of **those they lead**.

Spirit and belonging are travel companions. Each is nurtured and nourished by the other. Belonging is an inner feeling of comfort with space and time. To belong is to know that "I was meant to be here doing this work." Belonging is to be at the center of a wheel; the focal point of a journey that defines purpose, balance and a sense of connection with the other elements needed to move forward. Like the rim of the wheel, belonging is constantly being redefined by the forces and pressures that exist at the edge – the domain where our own learning is at its sharpest. The inner strength that flows from belonging is incomplete without a kinship with the other life forces on our planet: the changing of the seasons, plants, animals, nature, the environment. When the clay of belonging is lost as a life sustaining force, the spirit withers. To endure and grow as a leader is to be conscious of one's sense of belonging.

A prevailing thought in the mind of western culture is that much that ails us can be overcome if only we would spend more time *working on relationships*. Leadership, selling, love, marriage, personal growth, mentoring, self-doubt, so the mantra goes, all can be "fixed" if relationship skills are brought to the fore. The vast majority of such entreaties are empty vessels destined only to provide more noise and take up valuable emotional space in our lives. The self-help courses these works drum up are invariably of the head and the hand with little sense of the heart and the spirit. The capacity to build and thrive in intimacy is not a technique, or a set of skills to be learned, but a product and outcome of who we are. Intimacy is of the spirit. To be intimate is to give of ourselves without reservation. To be intimate with another we must first be intimate with ourselves. When we gaze into the mirror we must want to know the person who stares back at us. We must be willing to cast aside the masks we use to present ourselves to the world. We must develop the capacity to challenge the inner script that prompts us to act. We must be prepared to *stand naked* and look into the dark crevices of our inner-self. To know one's self is the secret of the master coach. To be open to input from others is a basic condition of sustainable leadership. To be aware of self is the first essential step in drawing richness out of the differences that separate us one from another. The leader's quest, when faced with resistance, conflict, or apathy, is not to try to mold or shape the behavior of others but to surface the discontent and to fill the space created with truth, integrity and authenticity.

Tension, contradiction and paradox fan the flames of spirit. The night is at its darkest just before the light of the dawn. The greatest beauty is that highlighted by a simple flaw. The prodigal son is the one who, upon his return, is asked to sit closest to the fire. The light from a candle is made more apparent by the shadows that it doesn't penetrate. Absolute silence makes the greatest sound. Success is most satisfying when the opponent is at the top of his/her game. The genesis of courage is not to be found in the heroic act, but in the spirit that enabled the performer to overcome his/her initial fear. The goals that generate the greatest degree of intensity are those thought to be beyond the capacity of the team. The coach is often at his/her most effective when he/she resists the need to intervene. Spirit in the warrior is made whole by the balance between the fierceness necessary to draw the bow and the gentleness demanded at the release of the arrow. Spirit in the leader is manifest in the toughness needed to constantly change the patterns of play and the empathy necessary to understand the needs and concerns of those involved in the work.

Fullness of spirit is the drumbeat of abundance. Autumn is a time when seeds planted during the spring and nourished by the warmth of the summer sun, give of their fruit. Autumn is the time of gathering and sharing. Autumn is a time of song. The spirit, as represented by the harvest, gives meaning to the planning initiated by the head, the planting orchestrated by the hand, and growth as embodied by the heart. Without an opportunity to harvest, the other seasons are merely harbingers of an empty promise. Harvest is a sacred time when *who gains* sets the emotional context for the next cycle of seasons. Leaders, real leaders, those who make a lasting difference, **bring in the harvest**.

There is little more noble than the mighty oak. It stands proud knowing that it has been a religious icon; the building block of empire; a shelter for the weak; and in the hands of the artist, a joy that lasts through the ages. The oak grows and flourishes not because of the primacy of one season but because of the balance between the seasons.

At first appearance our leadership oak appears strong and healthy. It stands tall and continues to grow. Can it be sick? We can't tell by looking more closely at what we see. We can't tell by listening to its mighty branches screaming in the gale. To know, we have to examine the roots. We must reach beyond the head and hand and touch the heart and spirit. Leadership is about balance. *Leadership lies not in any single skill or quality, but in the weave*. It is about the strategy of the head and the processes and systems that are of the hand. Without roots, however, the oak cannot survive. The first major storm, high wind, a drought, if the roots do not go deep this great mass will crash to the ground. Wisdom remains an untapped commodity, change initiatives falter, mergers fail, talent takes the mercenary path, and people become disillusioned when winter and spring are not complemented by the full flowering of summer and autumn.

The leader who wants to be the difference that makes a difference cannot depend on a root system that is shallow or fragile. Business people whose work is only of the head and the hand do not, in any substantive meaning of the word, deliver leadership. By the same token, leaders whose appeal is only of the heart and spirit are on a journey to nowhere. Leaders, real leaders, those who take people where they would otherwise not go, leaders who compete successfully for people's dreams *address the head, deliver the hand, engage the heart* **and** *enrich the spirit*.

Enjoy the flight!

Chapter Ten

Critical Learning

- Leadership balance is an imperative.
- Language and imagery touch the heart.
- Champions are nourished by the opportunity to move into new space.
- To share one's self is to engage the heart.
- Learning is of the heart.
- Spirit is anchored in a passionate desire to serve.
- The glue that bonds those in a great team is spirit.
- Spirit speaks of beliefs.

Consequences

Integration success is vital, but it is only the end of the beginning. To succeed in the longer term, the new executive needs to deliver leadership. Leadership, in turn, means engaging the heart and enriching the spirit. A focus on the head and hand exclusively and the new executive is severely limiting what is possible. In a post downsizing business world, the leader who does not address the "why" and "who gains" is mismanaging his or her most important resource.

Step back and reflect on the ideas that surfaced and the learning you take from this chapter. Consider the path you are on, the need to build relationships (fit), and your understanding of success in the new role (expectations). Think about what you need to stop doing, start doing, and that which you need to do differently.

_____

_____

_____

_____

_____

_____

_____

_____

_____

_____